law
and
poetry

Promises from the Preamble

Kristen David Adams
Editor

AMERICAN**BAR**ASSOCIATION

Business Law Section

Cover design by Catherine Zaccarine.

Printed in the United States of America.

25 24 23 22 21   5 4 3 2 1

ISBN: 978-1-63905-014-7

Discounts are available for books ordered in bulk. Special consideration is given to state bars, CLE programs, and other bar-related organizations. Inquire at Book Publishing, ABA Publishing, American Bar Association, 321 N. Clark Street, Chicago, Illinois 60654-7598.

www.shopABA.org

Table of Contents

Acknowledgments

So many people made this project possible, but it all started with my mother, Priscilla B. Adams. When I was young, I asked my mother about my middle name, David. She smiled and said, "I knew you would ask someday," and handed me a poem she had written entitled, "Poem for Pa." That poem, which was about my great-grandfather David Privette, was the beginning of my life-long love of poetry. My mother's example also inspired me to become an educator and author, as she was.

Shortly after I became a law professor in 2000, my mother and I were talking about a possible scholarly collaboration—this very anthology. She was the one who pointed me in the direction of Lincoln's first inaugural address, which inspired the framework for this book. Mom died in 2004, but I have carried this vision and these poems with me—metaphorically and sometimes literally—for the last twenty-plus years. The set of poems has changed over time, but the vision has always been to put together a set of poems that attempts to say something meaningful about the law.

I am thankful for the support of Stetson University College of Law as an institution—and for the support of so many colleagues. Michèle Alexandre, Dean of the College of Law, has given me opportunities to bring law and poetry into our campus conversations through the William Reece Smith, Jr. Distinguished Professorship and the support of the Joy McCann Foundation. The Dolly and Homer Hand Library and the Office of Faculty Support Services contributed countless hours of research and assisted in making contact with poets and their families all over the world. During my terms of service in law-school administration, my colleague Bob Bickel always urged me not to forget the things that brought me joy—or, in his words, "To find something I could get lost in the pure joy of doing." That *something* was always poetry. My colleague Brad Stone, who may enjoy poetry as much as I do, was a great inspiration, as well. Darby Dickerson encouraged me to envision a seminar class that would combine law and poetry. Stetson University Provost Noel Painter made it possible for me to teach that seminar on the DeLand campus, which in turn made it possible for me to spend countless happy afternoons in the poetry stacks of the DuPont-Ball Library. Kirsten Anderson has always sent me poems over the years that caught her eye. I have worked with outstanding research assistants who contributed excellent ideas and some favorite poems of their own, from Laura Vittetoe, who is now an accomplished attorney, to Sabrina Chianese, who just graduated and has a bright future ahead of her.

I will always be grateful to the American Bar Association Business Law Section—and especially Rick Paszkiet—for believing in this project. Rick, you and I have both believed that an anthology has something to contribute, even in the information age.

The greatest unexpected joy in this project has been communicating with poets and their families around the world. Their names are listed with the permissions they kindly gave. To a person, they have been gracious and responsive beyond any expectation. If these individuals are indicative of the modern world of poetry, it is robust, exciting, and dynamic. And in this age of division and mistrust, I am thankful and encouraged by the countless individuals who responded graciously to an out-of-the-blue message or letter from me—someone they did not know.

But the greatest thanks are to my family for participating in this journey with me for the last twenty-plus years. Dad, Susan, and Clay, thank you for supporting me in including one of Mom's poems. Jeff, thank you for your endless patience as I have obsessed over each and every poem and for sharing in my excitement as I celebrated each permission as it came in.

Preface

I am frequently asked why I believe there is a connection between law and poetry, and this is how I typically respond: A case or code helps to reveal what the law is. A treatise or law review article helps to reveal what the law perhaps should be. Poetry about the law, however, may be the single, most effective way to connect with the human experience of the law—by which I mean what it feels like to be the judge, the juror, the attorney, the witness, or even the accused. Some of the poems in this anthology were written by lawyers, some have obvious legal themes, and others illuminate legal concepts more obliquely. Many of the poets' names will be familiar, but I hope at least some will be new to each reader. Most of all, I hope this anthology will invite the exploration of new connections between law and poetry. The inspiration for this book comes from Abraham Lincoln's first inaugural address in 1861. The final paragraph of the address is as follows:

> I am loath to close. We are not enemies, but friends. We must not be enemies. Though passion may have strained it must not break our bonds of affection. The mystic chords of memory, stretching from every battlefield and patriot grave to every living heart and hearthstone all over this broad land, will yet swell the chorus of the Union, when again touched, as surely they will be, by the better angels of our nature.

In this address, Lincoln speaks at length about the future of the Union and how it might be preserved. In doing so, he states elsewhere in the address, "Continue to exercise all the express provisions of our National Constitution, and the Union will endure forever . . . ." As he acknowledges, one of the declared objects for ordaining and establishing the Constitution was "to form a more perfect Union."

With these thoughts in mind, and during this time in which the future of the Union is a matter of significant public discourse, it seemed appropriate to use the language from the Preamble to the Constitution as a means for presenting this anthology. This anthology consists of fifty-six poems, one for each state or commonwealth, the District of Columbia, and each of the five permanently inhabited territories that, together, comprise the United States of America. This collection of poems seeks to challenge the reader to consider how the promises and ideals of the Preamble might be fulfilled by "the better angels of our nature," and to illuminate opportunities for changes that might assist us in reaching those ideals.

We the People of the United States

As the United States is a country of more than 325 million people, the people of the United States are not easily described. The poems in this section provide just a few, illustrative snapshots of the people of the United States at our best, as well as showing areas of struggle. At our best, We the People of the United States seek to understand ourselves (and ultimately also one another) ("Hermit Crab"), and build connection and community with others who may seem unlike us ("Night Drive"). There is beauty, nobility, and inspiration to be found in the daily work of ordinary people ("My Brothers, Listen"). But We the People of the United States are also maddeningly fallible ("La Guerre") and often feel disconnected from the legal system that is to govern us ("The Laws of God, the Laws of Man"). On any given night in the United States, many of us experience homelessness ("Between Homes"), and we struggle with inclusivity and equity ("Ablesplaining Part 2,749").

✳ ✳ ✳ ✳ ✳

From a 2013 essay in the *Los Angeles Review of Books* entitled, "The Body of the Poem: On Transgender Poetry," by Stephanie Burt:

All of us are, like Doctor Who's TARDIS, bigger on the inside than on the outside. Few of us are finished, none of us ever find moments when we have at last enunciated the single, true, real, authentic, satisfactory self: instead, we can work to articulate that self as it changes and multiplies and evades us, whether or not we do so with our changing bodies' physical appearance, whether or not we do it in poems. "Who doesn't want / to be called something / other than the name we're given?" writes the contemporary poet Angie Estes. Nobody ever feels that even her closest friends know all of her, all the time, at any one time, and it only gets worse (we get more opaque) if we consider ourselves in time, since who I am now can obscure whatever I have been. Another contemporary poet, Laura Kasischke, writes that "growing older" is like being "blindfolded, walking // straight through one / immaterial mirror / and into another. / But it's never enough." You never see, you can never get other people to see, or hear, all of yourself: no one face, no one text, can suffice, no matter who you think you are. . . . . By writing poetry, by working in disembodied language, I can get out of the physical body I happen to have, can depict and counter the insufficiencies of the merely physical world; I can create other bodies for myself in words . . . ."

~   Hermit Crab

Stephanie Burt

That shell is pretty, but that shell is too small for me.

Each home is a hideout; each home is a secret; each home
is a getaway under the same hot lamp, a means
to a lateral move at low velocity.

I live in a room in the room
of a boy I barely see.

Sometimes the boy and his talkative friends raise
too-warm hands and try to set me free

and I retreat into myself, hoping they place
me back in my terrarium, and they
do, with disappointed alacrity.

Scatter patterns in sand, adnates, cancellates, gaping
whelk husks, a toy tractor-trailer, cracked
and dinged, beside the spine of a plastic tree,

the helmet-shaped shelter of a shadow cast
by a not-quite-buried wedge of pottery . . .

if I have a body that's wholly my own
then it isn't mine. For a while I was
protected by what I pretended to be.

Stephanie Burt was born in 1971 and is currently Professor of English and Director of Undergraduate Studies in Harvard University's Department of English. Dr. Burt earned her B.A. from Harvard University and her Ph.D. from Yale University. She is widely acclaimed, both as a poet and for leading the field of literary criticism for a generation. In this body of work, Dr. Burt has made it a priority to give readers the opportunity to become familiar with the works of less-known poets. The collection of poetry from which "Hermit Crab" comes was recognized as a National Endowment for the Arts Big Read; her essay collection *Close Calls with Nonsense* was a finalist for the National Book Critics Circle Award. Her *Don't Read Poetry: A Book About How to Read Poems* is a must-read for anyone who has ever felt intimidated by reading poetry. Her most recent book, *After Callimachus: Poems*, presents a new translation of an ancient Greek poet and was selected as one of the Top 10 Poetry Books of Spring 2020 by Publisher's Weekly.

From *Advice from the Lights* by Stephanie Burt. Minneapolis: Graywolf Press, 2017.

* * * * *

In the "Preliminary" to the collection of poems in which the poem below appears, the poet describes some of the influences for his work, which include the oral traditions, songs, and narrative verse of the Alaskan Eskimo, the Pueblo Indians of New Mexico, and the people of India. He also describes the longer poems, such as this one, as "lengthy stamens shaped to entrance the bee." As you read this poem, note how it draws you in and allows you to feel as though you are part of the experience. Also note the beauty and detail of the scene the poem creates, and remember that this poet is also an accomplished painter.

~   ## Night Drive, After a Workshop at the State Pen

John Brandi

> *Some poets equate themselves with criminals,*
> *maybe because we share the same desolate loves*
> —Richard Hugo

Drive away from the patrol towers
Drive through snowswirls down La Bajada Hill
Drive over transverse ridges, through far-off blink
    of blue-white towns in needling rain
Drive off the ramp, onto 44:   that same highway
       Eugene wrote about in class tonight: up through
          San Isidro, Cuba, Nageezi, doing 90
        in the penitentiary wagon, handcuffed in the dawn
          enroute to his brother's funeral.

Shift gears
Cross the bridge, feeling the river's invisible presence
    like a hand under me, as I remember steel bars
        and cell block grid patterns, the   SLAM
           of heavy doors between me and inmates
    in look-alike green: everybody reflected
        in giant fish-eye mirrors above walkie-talkie
          guards shouting codes from corridors
    to mess hall to impossible freedom
        of front-desk patrol-board doors.

Drive and avoid blinking detour signs
Drive, thinking of Rocky stroking his beard, guiding
    outrageous symphonic verse into "X-sharp major"
        saying: "to be a poet is to be an outlaw
          is to push things
             right to their limit."

Drive with my tank on empty
Drive not knowing   how far   how fast   how much fuel

Drive into questions without answers
       through dunes shifting to reveal
           another continent in the dark.

In Bernalillo I gas up
at the 7/11,   buy a sandwich from the girl
at Lottaburger, her top button missing, her fingers
      barely touching mine as she hands back the change.
I remember someone who held up a place like this
high on cocaine   — then got surprised
      by the spin of police lights; and spent
7 years waiting to be free, walking
the washed but never clean cell blocks, listening
to oldies but goodies, learning the art
         of blue tattoo; and the intricate weave
of used Camel cigarette-package picture frames.

Drive and accelerate to an even speed
Drive and swerve to miss dead skunks and hopping rabbits
Drive through flashes of lightning, remembering us there
      in the education wing: lifting shoulders
         tapping feet   to the raw-gut meter
        of unfinished verse:

Rudy, I see you struggling with that last line
about "*dos tecatos* in prayer," as if landing
      a 747 for the very first time.
And John, teaching me the correct form
of a Shakespearean sonnet, on a half-burnt table
      left over from the riot, telling me
"a wall can suddenly become a window
      opening into a place without rules"
         —where everyone lives outside the law
         —where skin has no color
           and birthdays have us all born
             on the same day.

And there is Willie
      his armed-robbery weightlifter hands
        delicately moving an Eagle Veriblack pencil
into faceless women, and "the leaking sound
        of time passing on"
his voice exclaiming: "Man, when I get out
      of this class, I'm up all night.
         I can't stop!"

Me, too, Willie.
I've had seven cups of coffee, and a wild drive

through snow and rain　—over a road I thought I knew well
but suddenly don't know at all. It strays
　　　　and threads over a lone mesa, then drops
　　　into sweet pungence of rotting apples
　　　　along orchard dikes that curve with the river.
I follow this road, mysteriously
　　　like how one of you described "following words
　　　　you have no understanding of, that sometimes open
　　　　　into walls to reveal doors
　　　that bring you home through a long dark tunnel."

Drive . . .
Drive and dip and juggle the road to miss potholes
Drive all the way home without feeling the wheel
Drive into my front yard, smell the odor
　　　of stacked cedar in the rain
　　　　—and suddenly get hit by the stars
　　　the 10,000 galaxies interconnected
　　　　　above your incarceration and my freedom;
　　　how you came out from behind bars
　　　　and I went in behind bars, to meet
　　　　　and make use of the power of the Word
　　　to bring back lost worlds
　　　　broken loves　　a child's voice
　　　　　or the silence
　　　　　　of a rain-shrouded mountain.

Drive, and stop
and realize　　　—tonight I have been somewhere
　　　　I have traveled to a place
　　　　　some people refuse to believe real
　　　　I have had tremendous fortune befall me
　　　　I have walked into a room full of company
　　　　I have come to know
　　　　　　another man.

John Brandi is an American poet and painter. Born in 1943, he is a native of Southern California and earned his B.A. in art and anthropology from California State University, Northridge. After serving in the Peace Corps in Ecuador from 1966 to 1968 and working with Quechua farmers who were struggling with land rights, Mr. Brandi returned to the United States, where he traveled, wrote, and continued the practice of keeping elaborate journals, which he had begun during his time in Ecuador. Mr. Brandi has traveled and taught extensively; his teaching has ranged from third grade through college and includes a number of teaching experiences in Native American schools, as well as lectures around the world. His collections of poetry number more than twenty-five, and draw on the wealth of experiences that began when he traveled with his parents in his youth. Mr. Brandi's paintings have been widely exhibited and, like his poetry, which draws in part on the West Coast Beat tradition, have garnered numerous honors.

From *Hymn for a Night Feast: Poems 1979–1986* by John Brandi. Stevens Point, Wisconsin: Holy Cow! Press, 1988.

* * * * *

This poem comes from a section of the book *Optimos* entitled, "The People are the Masters of Life." As you read this poem, note how this theme resounds throughout.

~ My Brothers, Listen

Horace Traubel

My brothers, listen, I have something to say to you:
I have watched you at your work through many days of
        many years,
I have shared with you your struggles for life and with your
        masters:
Now I ask you to listen, I want to make a confession.

I want to confess that I have taken my eyes off the kings
        and the great men and fixed them on you:
I have found in you what I expected to find in them and
        was cheated of,
I have hunted up reasons and roots and found them always
        in you,
I have read the great books and asked how they came and
        found they came from you:
The common man, the general earth, seas and stars, the
        unnamed, the immortally obscure.

You have threaded time and gone without returns,
You have always been where crises called for you, yet were
        never celebrated in the catalogue of events,
The kings have failed, the great have failed, you have never
        failed.

I saw that you fed the loom: but who fed you?
I saw that you fueled the fire: but who fueled you?
History put up big signs but they never bore your name,
History set great feasts but you were never invited.

You go to work in the morning with your dinner pail on
        your arm:

Does that pail contain your dinner alone and provide only
 for your simple day?
Millions of mouths to come hereafter are to be fed by that
 pail you carry on your arm.

When you go home at night after the day's work the universe
 goes home with you,
When you strike against the injustice of the master the sun
 strikes with you,
For streams run up and down from you, and the tides derive
 their ebb and flood from you,
For the pride of the world and the humility of the world
 are alike products of the muscles of your arms,
For the law of the common earth is the law of the common
 man.

My brother, listen, I have something to say to you:
I have arrived with the great world here at your workbench
 worshiping the tools of your trade,
I have adjourned all other causes to your cause and brought
 history close by to record your long ignored renown,
So that when men see you on your way to work mornings or
 nights or whenever they will take off their hats,
So that men and women and children will not go to church
 to see God or to the legislature to see Justice,
But will go to you wherever you are, in your humblest
 employment,
Hungry, confident, by you eternally confirmed.

Horace Logo Traubel (1858–1919) was an essayist, poet, publisher, and biographer, best known for his biography of Walt Whitman, his close friend for whom
he also served as literary executor. He was born in New Jersey and was closely
associated with the Arts and Crafts Movement in the United States. His formal
education ended at age twelve when he dropped out of school to assist his father,
who ran a stationery store. He founded the literary journal *The Conservator* and
was also associated with *The Artsman* for a time.

From *Optimos* by Horace Logo Traubel. New York: B.W. Huebsch, 1910.

* * * * *

The poem below is the first of five parts of "La Guerre" (the war). It was written
following the end of World War I, during which the poet served as a volunteer
ambulance driver in France. "La Guerre" is generally understood to capture many
of the poet's memories of the war in France.

~ La Guerre

e e cummings

I.

Humanity i love you
because you would rather black the boots of
success than enquire whose soul dangles from his
watch-chain which would be embarrassing for both

parties and because you
unflinchingly applaud all
songs containing the words country home and
mother when sung at the old howard

Humanity i love you because
when you're hard up you pawn your
intelligence to buy a drink and when
you're flush pride keeps

you from the pawn shop and
because you are continually committing
nuisances but more
especially in your own house

Humanity i love you because you
are perpetually putting the secret of
life in your pants and forgetting
it's there and sitting down

on it
and because you are
forever making poems in the lap
of death Humanity

i hate you

Edward Estlin Cummings (e e cummings) (1894–1962) wrote close to three thousand poems during his lifetime, in addition to several novels, plays, and essays. He is associated with modernist poetry and is considered one of the most influential modernist poets. He was born in Cambridge, Massachusetts, and received both his Bachelor of Arts and Master of Arts from Harvard University. During World War I, he served as a volunteer ambulance driver in France, was imprisoned for several months on suspicion of espionage and, shortly after his return to the United States, was drafted into service in the army. After the war, he traveled and wrote prolifically.

From *Tulips & Chimneys* by e e cummings. New York: Thomas Seltzer, Inc., 1923.

* * * * *

Housman has been described as a Romantic pessimist. As you read the lines below, however, you might consider whether they are pessimistic—or, instead, defiant in tone.

~ ## The Laws of God, the Laws of Man

A.E. Housman

The laws of God, the laws of man,
He may keep that will and can;
Not I: let God and man decree
Laws for themselves and not for me;
And if my ways are not as theirs
Let them mind their own affairs.
Their deeds I judge and much condemn,
Yet when did I make laws for them?
Please yourselves, say I, and they
Need only look the other way.
But no, they will not; they must still
Wrest their neighbour to their will,
And make me dance as they desire
With jail and gallows and hell-fire.
And how am I to face the odds
Of man's bedevilment and God's?
I, a stranger and afraid
In a world I never made.
They will be master, right or wrong;
Though both are foolish, both are strong.
And since, my soul, we cannot fly
To Saturn nor to Mercury,
Keep we must, if keep we can,
These foreign laws of God and man.

Alfred Edward (A.E.) Housman (1859–1936) was born in Worcestershire, England, attended St. John's College, Oxford, and held professorships in Latin at both University College, London and Trinity College, Cambridge, after having failed his final exams at Oxford and serving as a clerk in London's patent office for a decade. Housman published two volumes of poetry: the first was *A Shropshire Lad* and the second was *Last Poems,* in which the poem above appeared. It is said that Housman timed the publication of *Last Poems* so that his close friend and college roommate Moses Jackson, who was at the time dying in Canada, could read them in his last days.

From *Last Poems* by A.E. Housman. New York: Henry Holt and Company, 1922.

* * * * *

This poem originally appeared in the publication, *Street Sheet. Street Sheet* is an independent street newspaper dedicated to covering issues of homelessness and poverty in San Francisco from the voices of homeless people themselves.

~   Between Homes

Dee Allen.

About more times
Than I could count
All ten fingers
All ten toes,

I have lived
Between homes.

Existed in that
All too common
Space of homelessness
Indoors.

A friend's apartment,
A friend's company,
Their living room couch
Where I sought rest in the meantime,
Their wooden floor
Where my luggage sat,
Their lavatory where I
Cleansed my lean self
From wooly black head to toe
In the shower and
Shaved over their face-bowl,
Their kitchen where I warmed up
Or slapped together vegetarian
Miracles to please my tongue with.

A temporary arrangement
That had grown
Too old too soon,
Tested the limits
Of friendship,
Yielded no privacy

But time spent upon
A couch I'd visited
Often sure enough beats

The parking lot asphalt
Hard against your back,
The commands of harassing cops
GO! MOVE! KICK ROCKS!
The jail-like atmosphere
Of public shelters,
The shelter curfew
That traps you in at nightfall
And kicks you out at daybreak,
The fear of having your
Luggage stolen in your
Sleep by far needier hands,
The unspoken hate
In another's eyes
Upon seeing you carry
Luggage and sleeping-bag down
This street and that,
The unhoused condition outdoors,
The housed assume
Won't happen to them ——

About more times
Than I could count
All ten fingers
All ten toes,

I have lived
Between homes.

Existed in that
All too common
Space between
The last home
And the one
Home to come.
W: 4.19.17

Dee Allen is an African-Italian performance poet based in Oakland, California and active on the creative writing and Spoken Word scene since the early 1990s. He is the author of 5 books [Boneyard, Unwritten Law, Stormwater and Skeletal Black, all from POOR Press, and from Conviction 2 Change Publishing, Elohi Unitsi] and has 39 anthology appearances [including 2020: The Year That Changed America, Geography Is Irrelevant from York, England's Stairwell Books, Five Words: Volume XIV from West Cork, Ireland's O'Bheal, Boundless from Flower Song Press—created in connection to the 2021 Rio Grande Valley International Poetry Festival—and the newest from Kenya-based Kistrech Theatre International, I Can't Breathe] under his figurative belt so far.

From *Street Sheet*, edited by Quiver Watts. San Francisco: The Coalition on Homelessness, January 1, 2017.

*   *   *   *   *

This poem appeared in *We Are Not Your Metaphor: A Disability Poetry Anthology* edited by the Zoeglossia Fellows. Zoeglossia was established to provide an inclusive space for poets and authors who identify as disabled, and held its first conference in 2019. As you read this poem, you might consider the following words from the poet addressed to individuals with multiple cultural/social identities, which she shared on the topic of "writing for activists who don't fit in": "I believe now more than ever is the time for people to share their stories and to talk with one another about this world that we are co-creating. We may feel like we don't have any control or say in how it's being built, but I believe that reflection is one of our greatest tools in creating change. Reflecting on what we've tried, and what we want, gives us an opportunity to focus on the skills and tools we have already cultivated, instead of only focusing on what still needs to be fixed or what still needs to change."

~ **Ablesplaining**   **Part 2,749**

Naomi Ortiz

"Yes, we are a festival about celebrating and embracing diversity in our
community. No, we don't have a ramp for the stage . . . I don't see a problem
with having the founder of the festival MC from the ground. Besides, he's
the only person in a wheelchair that's part of the festival."
   When diversity is celebrated—except for disability.

   A festival about celebrating culture,
   that uses long plastic boxes pitched over winding electrical
       cords.
   Speed-bumps everywhere.

   I normally ram them at high speeds using momentum to slide
       over,
   but in the crowds, I must go slow,
   and I get stuck.
   The box is higher than the clearance of my scooter.
   I am stranded teetering on top, my wheels no longer
       touch the ground.

Abruptly, I am being shoved in the back—pushed out of my
    chair by some unknown person
        I can't see.
        I am being tipped to the side by a
        second man yanking on the scooter—I am falling—
            and I scream,

"STOP!"
No one listens.

"STOP TOUCHING ME!" I yell into the crowd of passing
    people.
No one listens.

Angrily, the man yanking on my scooter shouts, "WHAT! I
    was only trying to help!"
**His first time talking to me is a dismissal ablesplaining
    away my anger.**
But this gets into all the ways I am touched without consent.
My body taken over by a stranger.
**Where even when I'm yelling, surrounded by a crowd of
    people,
no one registers there's a problem.**

Naomi Ortiz is a Disabled Mestiza poet, visual artist, writer, speaker, and facil-
itator with a focus on a variety of subjects, including self-care, disability justice,
eco-justice, and intersectional organizing. She is the author of the non-fiction
book, *Sustaining Spirit: Self-Care for Social Justice*, a book for diverse communities
on dealing with the risks of burnout. Ortiz is highly active in social justice settings,
having directed National Kids as Self Advocates, a disability justice advocacy organization, as well as Help Increase the Peace and Alternatives to Violence, both of
which are anti-violence projects. She is a Zoeglossia Fellow, a National Association
of Latino Arts and Cultures Border Grant Narrative Awardee and has also offered
workshops to non-profits, youth groups, and individuals who are incarcerated.
The website www.NaomiOrtiz.com provides more information about Ortiz and
her work.

From *We Are Not Your Metaphor: A Disability Poetry Anthology*, edited by
Zoeglossia Fellows. Minneapolis, Minnesota: Squares and Rebels, 2019.

✳   ✳   ✳   ✳   ✳

in Order to form a more perfect Union

The United States consists of forty-six states, four commonwealths, five permanently inhabited territories, and the District of Columbia. The poems in this section explore what it would mean to form a more perfect union. This union, at its best, is one that honors the proud legacy of meaningful activism ("When I Rise Up") and values fraternity in the sense of fostering self-actualization ("True Freedom–How to Gain It"). Even so, this union struggles with the legacy of slavery ("A Curse for a Nation") and the Jim Crow laws ("Shall We Fight the Jim Crow Car?") as well as serious economic inequality ("To a Factory Whistle") and issues of fairness in the trial process ("The Mrichchakati") and the prison system ("The Ballad of Reading Gaol").

* * * * *

The poem below comes from the section of the collection *Bronze* entitled, "Exaltation." In a note at the beginning of *Bronze*, the poet stated as follows: "This book is the child of a bitter earth-wound. I sit on the earth and sing—sing out, and of, my sorrow. Yet, fully conscious of the potent agencies that silently work in their healing ministries, I know that God's sun will one day shine upon a perfected and unhampered people."

~ **When I Rise Up**

Georgia Douglas Johnson

When I rise above the earth,
And look down on the things that fetter me,
I beat my wings upon the air,
Or tranquil lie,
Surge after surge of potent strength
Like incense comes to me
When I rise above the earth
And look down upon the things that fetter me.

Georgia Douglas Johnson (1880–1966) was born in Atlanta, Georgia and was an African-American poet and playwright, as well as a teacher and an assistant principal in an Atlanta public school. She also wrote a syndicated newspaper column and was an important figure in the Harlem Renaissance, in part due to the "Saturday Salons" she hosted in her home for Langston Hughes, Alain Locke, Jean Toomer, and others. Johnson attended the Normal School at Atlanta University, which educated African-American women to become teachers during the time of segregation, and later studied music at Oberlin Conservatory of Music, which is credited as the oldest continuously operating conservatory in the United States. The poem above comes from her second collection of poems. Active in civil rights, Johnson was especially involved in the anti-lynching movement, as expressed in her plays. In 2009, she was inducted into the Georgia Writers Hall of Fame.

From *Bronze: A Book of Verse* by Georgia Douglas Johnson. Boston: B.J. Brimmer Company, 1922.

✳ ✳ ✳ ✳ ✳

This poem was published in the *Cambridge Chronicle*, founded in May 1846, which is the oldest surviving weekly newspaper in the United States. In considering the concept of *fraternity* and what true freedom is according to the narrator, also consider the following quote from Victor Hugo: "Great perils share this beauty, that they bring to light the fraternity of strangers."

~ True Freedom – How to Gain It

Charles MacKay

> We want no flag, no flaunting rag,
>> For liberty to fight, a
> We want no blaze of murderous guns,
>> To struggle for the right. a
> Our spears and swords are printed words,
>> The mind our battle plain; b
> We've won such victories before,
>> And hope we shall again. b
>
> We love no triumphs sprung of force,
>> They strain her brightest cause; c
> 'Tis not in blood that Liberty
>> Inscribes her civil laws. c
> She writes them on the people's hearts
>> In language clear and plain; b
> True thoughts that moved the world before,
>> And so they shall again. b
>
> We yield to none in earnest love
>> Of Freedom's cause sublime;
> We join the cry, "Fraternity!"
>> We keep the march of time,
> And yet we grasp no spike or spear,
>> Our victories to obtain;
> We've won without their aid before,
>> And so we shall again.

We want no aid of barricade,
    To show a front to wrong,
We want a citadel in truth,
    More durable and strong.
Calm words, great thoughts, unflinching faith,
    They've won our battles many a time,
And so they shall again.

[handwritten note: → changes the rhyme scheme to put emphasis on "faith" to lead the reader to believe that they can win.]

Peace, progress, knowledge, brotherhood –
    The ignorant may sneer,
The bad deny; but we rely
    To see their triumph near.
No widow's groans shall load our cause,
    No blood of brethren slain;
We've won without such aid before,
    And so we shall again.

Charles MacKay (1814–1889) was a Scottish journalist and poet. He held an LL.D from the University of Glasgow. He gained national recognition for his volume of poetry, *Voices from the Crowd*. His best-known work was *Memoirs of Extraordinary Popular Delusions and the Madness of Crowds*, which is still in print, although the title has varied a bit over the years.

From *Cambridge Chronicle*, Vol. VIII, No. 47. Cambridge, Massachusetts: November 19, 1853.

* * * * *

Although at the time believed by many to be a denunciation of Browning's native England for its policy of military non-intervention, this poem, which appeared in *The Liberty Bell* in Boston in 1856, is now understood to have been aimed at slavery in the United States. *The Liberty Bell* was an annual publication by a group of abolitionists, all female, to raise money for the abolitionist cause. As you read this poem, note how the meter and rhyme scheme of the poem change from the Prologue to the Curse, and how these contribute to the experience of reading the poem.

~ A Curse for a Nation

Elizabeth Barrett Browning

Prologue

I heard an angel speak last night,
    And he said, "Write!
Write a Nation's curse for me,
And send it over the Western Sea."

I faltered, taking up the word:
  "Not so, my lord!
If curses must be, choose another
To send thy curse against my brother.

"For I am bound by gratitude,
  By love and blood,
To brothers of mine across the sea,
Who stretch out kindly hands to me."

"Therefore," the voice said, "shalt thou write
  My curse to-night.
From the summits of love a curse is driven,
As lightning is from the tops of heaven."

"Not so," I answered. "Evermore
  My heart is sore
For my own land's sins: for little feet
Of children bleeding along the street:

"For parked-up honors that gainsay
  The right of way:
For almsgiving through a door that is
Not open enough for two friends to kiss:

"For love of freedom which abates
  Beyond the Straits:
For patriot virtue starved to vice on
Self-praise, self-interest, and suspicion:

"For an oligarchic parliament,
  And bribes well-meant.
What curse to another land assign,
When heavy-souled for the sins of mine?"

"Therefore," the voice said, "shalt thou write
  My curse to-night.
Because thou hast strength to see and hate
A foul thing done *within* thy gate."

"Not so," I answered once again.
  "To curse choose men.
For I, a woman, have only known
How the heart melts, and the tears run down."

"Therefore," the voice said, "shalt thou write
  My curse to-night.
Some women weep and curse, I say,
(And no one marvels) night and day.

"And thou shalt take their part to-night,
    Weep and write.
A curse from the depths of womanhood
Is very salt, and bitter, and good."

So thus I wrote, and mourned indeed,
    What all may read.
And thus, as was enjoined on me,
I send it over the Western Sea.

The Curse

I.

Because ye have broken your own chain
    With the strain
Of brave men climbing a nation's height,
Yet thence bear down with brand and thong
On souls of others, — for this wrong
    This is the curse. Write.

Because yourselves are standing straight
    In the state
Of Freedom's foremost acolyte,
Yet keep calm footing all the time
On writhing bond-slaves, — for this crime
    This is the curse. Write.

Because ye prosper in God's name,
    With a claim
To honor in the old world's sight,
Yet do the fiend's work perfectly
In strangling martyrs, — for this lie
    This is the curse. Write.

II.

Ye shall watch while kings conspire
Round the people's smouldering fire,
    And, warm for your part,
Shall never dare — O shame!
To utter the thought into flame
    Which burns at your heart.
        This is the curse. Write.

Ye shall watch while nations strive
With the bloodhounds, die or survive,
    Drop faint from their jaws,
Or throttle them backward to death;

And only under your breath
Shall favor the cause.
This is the curse. Write.

Ye shall watch while strong men draw
The nets of feudal law
To strangle the weak;
And, counting the sin for a sin,
Your soul shall be sadder within
Than the word ye shall speak.
This is the curse. Write.

When good men are praying erect
That Christ may avenge his elect
And deliver the earth,
The prayer in your ears, said low,
Shall sound like the tramp of a foe
That's driving you forth.
This is the curse. Write.

When wise men give you their praise,
They shall praise in the heat of the phrase,
As if carried too far.
When ye boast your own charters kept true,
Ye shall blush; for the thing which ye do
Derides what ye are.
This is the curse. Write.

When fools cast taunts at your gate,
Your scorn ye shall somewhat abate
As ye look o'er the wall:
For your conscience, tradition, and name
Explode with a deadlier blame
Than the worst of them all.
This is the curse. Write.

Go, wherever ill deeds shall be done,
Go, plant your flag in the sun
Beside the ill-doers!
And recoil from clenching the curse
Of God's witnessing Universe
With a curse of yours.
This is the curse. Write.

Elizabeth Barrett Browning (1806–1861) was a leading poet of the Victorian era. Barrett Browning opposed slavery, and "A Curse for a Nation" reflects this position. Ironically, Barrett Browning's father was an enslaver for many years. In 1846,

Barrett Browning married the poet Robert Browning and suffered disinheritance as a result. Barrett Browning continued to write and publish poetry, interacting with many leading poets and writers of her day. Her literary circle included at various points William Wordsworth, Thomas Carlyle, Samuel Taylor Coleridge, William Makepeace Thackeray, John Ruskin, and Alfred, Lord Tennyson.

Reprinted in *Best-Known Poems of Elizabeth and Robert Browning*. New York: The Book League of America, 1942.

* * * * *

Following the formal abolition of slavery in 1865 with the Thirteenth Amendment, the Jim Crow laws were put in place. As you read this poem, you might consider the various forms that the "color-bar" has taken in the United States over time.

~ Shall We Fight the Jim Crow Car?

Carrie Williams Clifford

[handwritten note: rhyme sounds like a train / drives you forward]

Comes the question, loud, insistent,
Borne upon the winds afar,
In the ears of black men ringing—
"Shall we fight the Jim Crow car?"

Mounts the hot blood to the forehead,
Angry passions leap to life
At remembered wrongs committed
'Gainst a mother, sister, wife.

And the milk of human kindness
In the proud heart turns to gall:
Is not every hand against them,
Every ear deaf to their call?

Disregarded all entreaties,
Stern protests unheeded are;
Impotent words or achievements,
To remove the color-bar.

Shall such base, unworthy treatment
Be by brave men tamely borne
And the title "Non-resistant,"
As a badge of honor worn?

No; by heaven, they swear it, swear it!
List ye, farthest glitt'ring star,
Ten thousand black men shout in chorus,
"We will fight the Jim Crow car."

Carrie Williams Clifford (1882–1934) was a committed activist and poet. She was married to William H. Clifford, a lawyer and member of the Ohio State Legislature. In 1901, she co-founded the Ohio Federation of Colored Women's Clubs. As the president of this organization, Clifford was a vocal and ardent supporter of women's suffrage and racial equality. Upon the founding of the NAACP in 1910, Clifford occupied a key leadership role. She died in 1934.

From *Race Rhymes* by Carrie Williams Clifford. Washington, D.C.: R.L. Pendleton, 1911.

* * * * *

The poem below was published in the *Industrial Pioneer*, a monthly publication of the Industrial Workers of the World that ran from February 1921 to September 1926. The IWW is a labor organization (the members of which are known colloquially as the Wobblies) founded in 1905 in Chicago. The IWW's logo bears the words, "Labor is entitled to all it produces." As you read the poem below, you might consider these words.

~ To a Factory Whistle

S.P.

O grim-voiced Demon, soulless Monster, why
Must I your summons heed, nor fail to come,
When you would call me back to toil, while some
Loiter along the way? Is your hoarse cry
For me alone? May these stand idle by,
Yet take the loaf and leave to me the crumb?
Surely! Justice is dead, or else turned dumb:
Why does my brother loiter and not I?
Or why, with bended back and pain-wracked frame,
Must I, for these long, weary hours each day,
Stifle both sense and soul? Is it that he
May live and labor not? Justice? A name!
I toil that both may live and he may play.
Why are things so? Grim Monster, answer me!

The identity of S.P. is unknown, although one can assume that the poet was most likely a member of the Industrial Workers of the World.

From *Industrial Pioneer*, Vol. 1, No. 6 (July 1921) by the Industrial Workers of the World, Chicago.

* * * * *

The lines below were excerpted from the play, *The Mrichchakati*, or *The Toy Cart: A Drama*. This Sanskrit drama in ten acts is attributed to Śūdraka, an ancient playwright. The lines that appear below were spoken by Chárudatta, a noble Brahmin who had given all of his belongings to the poor and thus impoverished himself. In this scene, Chárudatta, who has been falsely accused of murder, enters the courtroom where he is to be tried. He speaks the following words in response to the Officer's saying to him, "This is the court, Sir, enter."

~   ### *From* The Mrichchakati (or The Toy Cart), Act IX, The Hall of Justice

Śūdraka

> The prospect is but little pleasing.
> The court looks like a sea – its councillors
> Are deep engulphed in thought; its tossing waves
> Are wrangling advocates; its brood of monsters
> Are these wild animals—death's ministers—
> Attorneys skim like wily snakes the surface—
> Spies are the shell fish cowering 'midst its weeds,
> And vile informers, like the hovering curlew
> Hang fluttering o'er, then pounce upon their prey:
> The bench, that should be justice, is unsafe,
> Rough, rude, and broken by oppression's storms.

Śūdraka was an Indian king to whom three Sanskrit plays are ascribed. He lived between the second century B.C. and the fifth century A.D. Little is known of how ancient Indian plays were performed since no playhouse has survived, although some scholars have surmised that the stage was likely raised and supported with pillars, and little or no scenery was employed.

From *The Mrichchakati*, or *The Toy Cart: A Drama*, trans. by Horace Hayman Wilson, Esq. Calcutta: Asiatic Press, 1826.

*   *   *   *   *

Her Majesty's Prison Reading, formerly known as Reading Gaol, was built in 1844 and closed in 2014. Oscar Wilde was inspired to write the poem below after an execution during his imprisonment there. Wilde's imprisonment resulted from charges of "gross indecency" on Wilde's part based on evidence of Wilde's relationships with men. This poem was Wilde's last work, first published in 1898 about 2 years before he died at age 46. The poem was published under "C.3.3" rather than Wilde's name, to denote the cell block and number where Wilde was held. The excerpt below is from part V of this six-part work. The total work consisted of 109 six-line stanzas.

~ *From* The Ballad of Reading Gaol

Oscar Wilde

I know not whether Laws be right,
   Or whether Laws be wrong; a
All that we know who lie in gaol
   Is that the wall is strong; a
And that each day is like a year,
   A year whose days are long. a

But this I know, that every Law
   That men have made for Man, b
Since first Man took his brother's life,
   And the sad world began, b
But straws the wheat and saves the chaff
   With a most evil fan. b

This too I know—and wise it were
   If each could know the same— c
That every prison that men build
   Is built with bricks of shame, c
And bound with bars lest Christ should see
   How men their brothers maim. c

Oscar Wilde (1854–1900) was an Irish poet and playwright, enjoying considerable success as a late Victorian playwright. Wilde's popularity took a dramatic downturn after his arrest, conviction, and imprisonment for what was termed at the time gross indecency in 1895 after two controversial trials—one of which concerned Wilde's private prosecution of the Marquess of Queensberry for libel. Notably, during Wilde's suit against the Marquess, the defense attorney engaged in a lengthy cross-examination of Wilde, with the content of Wilde's poetry and his private life at issue. The evidence of Wilde's relationships with men that emerged during the libel trial led to subsequent charges against Wilde for gross indecency, for which he was imprisoned for two years. Wilde spent his post-prison life in France, where he died at the age of 46, destitute and ruined from the publicity of his arrest and conviction. He was posthumously pardoned in 2017 under the Policing and Crime Act of 2017, fifty years after decriminalization was begun in England and Wales.

From *The Poems of Oscar Wilde*. London: Methuen and Co., 1908.

* * * * *

How the criminal justice system treats drug convictions / how it contributes to the nation-wide issue of addiction / overdose

Establish Justice

Aleksandr Solzhenitsyn saw justice as conscience, not in the limited sense of a personal conscience, but rather as a societal conscience of all of humanity. This section explores justice in both the personal sense and the broader societal sense. It begins and ends with poems in the epigram style, Walt Whitman's "Thought" and Robert Herrick's "Lawes." These are intended, respectively, to invoke the vastness of the concept of justice and its inherent relationship to equality, and its ability to defeat tyranny. Between these two bookends are poems that illustrate the desire to establish justice—as in "2009 Criminal Docket," and how our system of justice has struggled with respect to persons of color ("Injustice of the Courts") and society's most vulnerable ("Offerings to an Ulcerated God" and "Baby's First Bath"). The penultimate poem in this section, "School Bus Wreck," presents a circumstance—the loss of children's lives in a horrible accident—in which truly meaningful justice is difficult to accomplish.

* * * * *

Epigram style

These four poems, each entitled "Thought," are interspersed with others in the portion of *Leaves of Grass* entitled, "By the Roadside." Each was written in 1860. As you read these poems, you might consider what they each suggest about the relationship between law, justice, and equality.

~ Thought

Walt Whitman

Of Justice—as if Justice could be any thing but the same ample law,
    expounded by natural judges and saviors,
As if it might be this thing or that thing, according to decisions.

~ Thought

Walt Whitman

Justice stands eternal under Higher Law, aloof from whim of jury or magistrate.

~ Thought

Walt Whitman

Of Equality—as if it harm'd me, giving others the same chances and
      rights as myself—as if it were not indispensable to my own rights
      that others possess the same.

~ Thought

Walt Whitman

Only when your chances and rights are equal to mine does my well
being flourish.

Walt Whitman (1819–1892) was an American poet and essayist. He was an iconic
figure in American transcendentalism and a leader in the utilization of free verse.
Whitman published the first edition of *Leaves of Grass* at his own expense, selling a house to generate the funds to do so. The poems are not arranged in the
order in which they were composed, and Whitman constantly changed poems'
titles and moved poems around in the nine editions that were published while
he was alive.

From Walt Whitman's *Complete Leaves of Grass*, edited by William L. Moore.
Tokyo: Taibundo, 1966.

* * * * *

Michael J. Howlett, Jr. became a judge in 2005, sitting in the Criminal Division
of the Circuit Court of Cook County, Illinois. Among other accomplishments, he
served as Deputy Special Outside Counsel to the U.S. House of Representatives
Ethics Committee and as an officer and director of the Lawyers Assistance
Program. As you read the poem below, think through what Judge Howlett has told
us about each defendant, their background, the charge, and the plea or verdict.

~ 2009 Criminal Docket

Michael J. Howlett, Jr.

Monday's Docket

All rise
His Honor
No talking

Sheet 4 Line 4
Male 24

Eighth grade
2 felony priors
Robbery $14.68
Agreed Plea
4 years IDOC*

Sheet 3 Line 5
Male 43
Junior college
Sex offender
Registration violation
Plea
2 years IDOC

Sheet 10 Line 2
Male 18
6th grade
Armed robbery
Bodily harm
Bench Trial
5yrs IDOC

Adjourn

Tuesday's Docket

All ri . . .
Tuesday's Prayer

Abide with me,
And
From the chill of nonchalance,
Safeguard my soul.

*Illinois Department of Corrections (Howlett's footnote)

Michael J. Howlett, Jr. (1948–2014) was a felony trial judge. During his impressive career, he was a defense attorney, a prosecutor, and a litigator at a major Chicago firm. From 1977 to 2010, he taught law courses at Loyola University (Chicago) and the University of Chicago.

From 36 Legal Stud. F. 273 (2012).

✳   ✳   ✳   ✳   ✳

In reading this poem, which was written during the Jim Crow era that began shortly after the Civil War, you might consider in what way or from what perspective have the jurors "legalized the lynchers."

~ Injustice of the Courts

Lizelia Augusta Jenkins Moorer

Whites alone upon the jury in a number of the states,
Thus they crush a helpless Negro with their prejudicial hates;
Legal ills they thrust upon him, and the tale is passing sad—
Equal rights with white men? Never! Color-phobia makes them mad.

'Tis the training of the children, every Negro to suppress,
They their spleen may vent upon him and be happy, none the less,
They will boast aloud in anger if by Negroes they are crossed,
"If we shoot or kill a Negro, not a cent will be the cost."

Juries represent the people and their sentiments make known,
When a Negro comes in question there's discrimination shown.
They are bold to make assertion that they will not do the same
For a Negro as a white man, and no feeling comes of shame.

Jurymen have made confession after trial had been made
Of a Negro, and "He's guilty!" was the verdict there displayed.
Stern remorse so touched the conscience, they the story did relate,
How the verdict they had rendered was to stay the dying fate.

"It was hard to say him guilty, for the man, we thought, was clear.
But a mob was making clamors that were terrible to hear."
"Punishment or death!" it shouted, and around began to press;
And of two impending evils, we have chosen him the less.

Thus we legalized the lynchers, we their words to court have brought,
And the innocent convicted! how revolting is the thought!
When a mob has forced a jury to a stand against the right,
All the waters of the ocean cannot make the conscience white.

Once a Negro girl was saucy, and the wife the husband told,
Who in haste arraigned the servant and began to swear and scold.
Then he whipped her without mercy—straightway she to law applied.
Passing strange—they found him guilty, and the judge was sorely tried.

This he said, in making sentence, "No disfavor comes to you,
You have only done as others, or as I myself would do,
If your servants vex the mistress, thrash them out again, I say,
Go to jail ten minutes only, and a fine of five cents pay!"

If a judge is conscientious, then the people vote him out,
His partiality to white men they must know, beyond a doubt.
No equality for Negroes in the law the world must know,
If he fails to make distinctions, from the bench they'll have him go.

This injustice is a cancer, in the nation's breast it lives,
Quietly and unmolested, awful is the death it gives.
It results from color-phobia, which the God of right defies,
Slaves of prejudice, take warning! pause before the nation dies.

All the land is running riot, laws are trampled in the face,
Negroes must be law-abiding; whites alone the laws debase.
Wrong upon itself is coiling, hissing serpent of the times,
Whites in self-defense are crying, "Shield us from our people's crimes."

Barbarism fills the country, all for safety take alarm,
From the lowest to the highest, no one now is free from harm;
Anarchy is rife among us, all resulting from the same,
Gross injustice of the court-room brings the nation into shame.

Lawlessness is at a premium, woeful penalty it brings,
Relic of the middle ages is the present state of things.
To the winds we now are sowing, and the whirl-wind comes at length,
Evils cast upon the waters come again with added strength.

Lizelia Augusta Jenkins Moorer (1868–1936) used her poems to attack issues faced by fellow black Americans, including Jim Crow laws, the church's hypocrisy, debt peonage, the press, and lynching. She was a teacher as well as a poet and an active member of the Woman's Christian Temperance Union. She was born in Pickens, South Carolina and married Jacob Moorer, an attorney in Orangeburg, South Carolina, where they lived. She attended Claflin University, the oldest historically black college or university in South Carolina.

From *Prejudice Unveiled: and Other Poems* by Lizelia Augusta Jenkins Moorer. Boston: Roxburgh Publishing Company, 1907.

✳ ✳ ✳ ✳ ✳

Martín Espada published his first book of poems shortly before he began law school. In a 2015 interview with *Sampsonia Way*, he shared some of his experiences as both a tenant attorney and a poet: "I used to sit on the stairs outside the courtroom, and scratch out poems on legal pads while I was waiting for our cases to be called. There were juvenile hearings prior to the housing cases, and, of course, given their right to privacy we were not allowed inside the courtroom while that was going on. Everyone was in the hallway or on the stairs. I sat there. I wrote poems. It was not as crazy as it might sound because, whether I was working or am working as a lawyer or a poet, I am an advocate. I am speaking on behalf of others without an opportunity to be heard. At that time and place, they happened to be people in the community of Chelsea and beyond." Consider this context as you read the poem below.

~   **Offerings to an Ulcerated God**
Chelsea, Massachusetts

Martín Espada

Mrs. López refuses to pay rent,
and we want her out,
the landlord's lawyer said,
tugging at his law school ring.
The judge called for an interpreter,
but all the interpreters were gone,
trafficking in Spanish
at the criminal session
on the second floor.

A volunteer stood up in the gallery.
Mrs. López showed the interpreter
a poker hand of snapshots,
the rat curled in a glue trap
next to the refrigerator,
the water frozen in the toilet,
a door without a doorknob.
(No rent for this. I know the law
and I want to speak,
she whispered to the interpreter).

Tell her she has to pay
and she has ten days to get out,
the judge commanded, rose
so the rest of the courtroom rose,
and left the bench. Suddenly
the courtroom clattered
with the end of business:
the clerk of the court
gathered her files
and the bailiff went to lunch.
Mrs. López stood before the bench,
still holding up her fan of snapshots
like an offering this ulcerated god
refused to taste,
while the interpreter
felt the burning
bubble in his throat
as he slowly turned to face her.

Martín Espada was born in Brooklyn, New York in 1957. He follows his father's tradition of civic engagement and pursuit of social justice; Frank Espada, a community organizer and documentary photographer, created the Puerto Rican

Diaspora Documentary Project. Martín Espada earned his B.A. from the University of Wisconsin-Madison, his J.D. from Northeastern University, and practiced as a tenant lawyer and supervisor of Su Clínica Legal, a legal services program for low-income, Spanish-speaking tenants in Chelsea, Massachusetts, outside Boston. A poet, social-justice activist, editor, essayist, and translator, Espada has written more than twenty books and currently teaches English at the University of Massachusetts-Amherst. His numerous honors include a Guggenheim Foundation Fellowship, an Academy of American Poets Fellowship, and the 2018 Ruth Lilly Poetry Prize.

From *Imagine the Angels of Bread* by Martín Espada, New York: W.W. Norton & Company, 1996.

✳ ✳ ✳ ✳ ✳

As you read this heart-wrenching poem, note how the title belies the terrible account that follows, and consider the efforts by the police officer, the social worker, and the attorney to pursue justice on the infant's behalf.

~ Baby's First Bath

Nancy A. Henry

The dead infant
is scalded white and scarlet
a horrible piebald fish.

Beside me at counsel table,
the gentle social worker who found him
the cop on the stand
who took the picture,
breaking down.

Do you need a moment officer?
No, I'll go on. I can go on.

No inept parent's failure caused this
though I'm sure the careful warnings
were a helpful guide
to what was done so awfully well.

There is enough ugliness you will live to see
without my putting this dead baby
in your head.

Forgive me.
He cried so much in my sleep
I thought he needed more people
to hear him.

Nancy A. Henry was born in Chipley, Florida in 1961, grew up in Gainesville, Florida, and now lives in Gloucester, Massachusetts. She is a poet and a collage artist and, in what she describes as her former life as an attorney, practiced in the field of child protection. She has taught English and Humanities at four colleges and universities. Her work includes five chapbooks and three full-length collections of poetry, including one, *Who You Are*, which focuses on her legal and child advocacy work. Two of her poems have been featured on Garrison Keillor's *Writer's Almanac*. Honors for her poetry include an Atlanta Review International Merit Award and four Pushcart Prize nominations.

From *Anything Can Happen* by Nancy A. Henry. New York: Muscle Head Press, 2002.

* * * * *

As you read the poem below, written by a life-long teacher, you might consider the following quotation by Barbara Charline Jordan (1936-1996), which the poet chose for an inscription in the seventh grade girls' locker commons at the school where she taught for twenty-nine years: "I have faith in young people because I know the strongest emotions that prevail are those of love and caring and belief and tolerance."

~ School Bus Wreck

Priscilla B. Adams

The sun sifts through the trees
On a cool, foggy September morning,
On the winding backroad,
On a yellow pencil on black pavement
And on cold, empty seats and silent aisles;
On a concrete bridge, on grass and blood,
On books and apples;
On a silent crowd gathered around,
Mangled like the bus,
Like the lives of those who survived,
Who were cheated out of
The promise of children who died.

Priscilla B. Adams (1944–2004) taught English at The Westminster Schools in Atlanta, Georgia. She was appointed to the faculty in 1975, received the Alumni Fellows Distinguished Teaching Award, held the Lane Chair of English from 1995 to 1999, and served as English department chair from 1999 until her death. She was a Phi Beta Kappa graduate of the University of North Carolina at Chapel Hill and earned her Masters degree from Drake University. She published two books, *Thinking on Paper: A Guide to Writing and Revising*, and *Poetry Windows and Mirrors: A Sketchbook Approach to Writing and Reading Poetry*.

From *Poetry Windows and Mirrors: A Sketchbook Approach to Writing and Reading Poetry* by Priscilla B. Adams. Durham: Carolina Academic Press, 1995.

* * * * *

Epigram Style This poem is written in the style of an epigram. The epigram style has come to be associated with short, pithy verse, and especially that which purports to communicate some moral point. As you read this poem, you might consider how, according to the poem, law can defeat tyranny.

~ **Lawes**

Robert Herrick

When Lawes full power have to sway, we see
Little or no part there of Tyrannie.

Robert Herrick (1591–1674) was a seventeenth-century English poet born in London. Prior to his education at the University of Cambridge, he was apprenticed to his uncle, a wealthy goldsmith. Herrick was a supporter of the king during the English Civil War and an English vicar. He lost his position as vicar for fourteen years due to his political convictions and his support of Charles I. When Charles II came to power in 1660, he was reinstated.

From *The Complete Poems of Robert Herrick, Volume 2.* London: Chatto & Windus, 1876.

* * * * *

insure domestic Tranquility

In this section, which is meant to be experienced as a reflective pause, we reach the midpoint of the book. Domestic tranquility can be understood as peace at home, a concept that can have a number of meanings. In exploring this concept, the first poems in this section build from personal situations that challenge domestic tranquility to broader societal matters. In doing so, "Vacation" explores the tension between work and family time, while "Letters of Credit" examines the complexity of family relationships. "From an 'L' Train Window" explores themes of poverty and isolation. Abraham Lincoln's untitled poem evokes the feeling of missing home. "The White House" explores what it means to feel unwelcome and unsafe. "The Subalterns" addresses sickness and death. Ending this section, "Going Home" invokes the concept of "home" in a broader, more universal sense.

* * * * *

The collection of poems in which the poem below appears is dedicated to "everyone who persists in the practice of law." The collection begins with sections entitled "Opening Statement" and "Law School" and proceeds through a number of stages of law practice to its closing sections, "Disillusionment: The Limericks" and "Closing Argument." The poem below appears in the section entitled, "Life in the Firm."

~ Vacation

J.D. DuPuy and M.L. Philpott

first night at the beach.
surf sounds and a cool, cleansing breeze
have brought forgiveness from loved ones
for not leaving the office sooner this morning.
innumerable stars give the appearance of a vast,
distant city in the otherwise black sky.
ghost crabs peek out from their holes in the sand near where I stand,
breathing.

[BUZZ]

a sudden, invasive brightness frightens them back underground.

[BUZZ]

the harsh light spreads into the night air.
stars fade.

no. not [BUZZ] now.

it's no use to hope for spam.
the office center by the check-in desk in the lobby awaits,
tinted glass allowing in
judgmental stares from disbelieving vacationers.

three days have passed.
one meal and a half with my family and a short trip to the alligator farm
and that's it,
but it could have been worse.
all is not lost.
one day remains.
but first, sleep – it is late.

the waves pound and recede.
the sheets – have they been this soft all week? – fold closed around me.
sleep
　　　　　pulls
　　　　　　　　me
　　　　　　　　　　　under.
[BUZZ]

a blue glow fills the room.

Mary Laura Philpott lives in Nashville, Tennessee and is the bestselling author of *I Miss You When I Blink* and *Bomb Shelter*. Her work is featured frequently by the *New York Times* and also appears in the *Atlantic*, the *Washington Post*, the *Paris Review Daily*, and other publications. She has won an Emmy for her work on *A Word On Words*, a Nashville Public Television literary series about books and authors.

James D. DuPuy is an attorney in Charlotte, North Carolina. He practices estate administration, tax foreclosure, and commercial real estate law. He is also active in the community, serving in leadership positions for both The Salvation Army of Greater Charlotte and Friends of Acción, the latter of which benefits the Mayan people in Mexico's Yucatan peninsula.

DuPuy and Philpott have been friends since both were students at Davidson College, and collaborated in creating *Poetic Justice: Legal Humor in Verse*.

From *Poetic Justice: Legal Humor in Verse* by J.D. DuPuy and M.L. Philpott. Poetic Justice, LLC, 2013.

✶　✶　✶　✶　✶

This poem speaks of the currency of relationships. A letter of credit is generally considered to be the most secure means of payment in commerce, especially in a situation in which there is great distance and no relationship of trust (such as a first transaction between parties in different countries with no prior dealings with one another). In reading this poem, you might consider how the analogy plays out between the protagonist and his children. What is "the debt" to which the poem refers? Is there any question of remorse or is the account simply closed?

~   **Letters of Credit**

Steven M. Richman

He looks deeply into the mirror of his children
but cannot see himself, though he knows he is there,
somewhere in the depths. They speak to him
with the greatest politeness, and if there is affection
he feels it as the slightest warm breeze in summer,
a hot dying breath of presence, not of comfort.

He works their love like his job, studying precedent
and applying law to fact, to derive a holding, a balance
of truth, justice and equity, completely anomalous
in the calculus of emotion. Still there is a sense of obligation,
like throwing coins into the tollbooth — regardless of whether
they hit, or bounce off the rim and roll away, the debt is paid.

They are gone, glimpsed through materializing letters
on the instant messaging boards of computer screens,
or in the electronic conversions of voices to ear, heard
like the ocean in shell: false, imitative, distant and faint,
or like letters of credit, carrying his value into the void
of commerce, of life, to distant lands he will never see.

Steven M. Richman is admitted to practice in New Jersey, Pennsylvania, New York, and California. Richman's areas of practice include domestic and international commercial law, intellectual property (including art and photography law), and mediation, arbitration, and litigation. He has held a number of leadership roles within the International Bar Association and the American Bar Association, having served as Chair of the ABA's International Law Section, a long-time member of the ABA's House of Delegates, and Chair of the IBA's Credentials Committee, among other leadership roles. Richman has been part of the IBA's Presidential Taskforce, examining the root causes of what has been termed the current crisis in attorney wellbeing. He is also an accomplished photographer and the author of *The Photography Law Handbook*, published by the ABA, and four books of photographs.

From 36 Legal Stud. F. 339 (2012).

∗ ∗ ∗ ∗ ∗

"Quarter Lodgers" seems to be a term the poet has coined. As you read this poem, you might consider what this term means in this context, as well as the symbolism of the elevated train.

~   From an 'L' Train Window

Dana Burnet

I saw bent figures toiling in a dusk
  That seemed beyond the reaches of the Day,
Pinched faces at the grimy window squares,
  Youth turned to something wracked and old and gray.

I had left sunshine on my study floor,
  Laughter behind me in a woman's eyes,
Paintings and books and friendly smiling things,
  The sum of which is mortal paradise.

Yet here in that same world bent figures toiled
  From gloomy windows to the deeps of gloom,
Thin-fingered women, sad as prisoners,
  Plied glinting needles in a coffin'd room.

The Quarter Lodgers, sprawled upon a bench,
  Read crumpled paper in the half-slain light,
Draining the sordid romance of the press,
  Finding some little comfort from their plight.

And then a child, with eyes to break my heart
  Leaned from a window and with hands that shook
Poured water on a dead geranium –
  And that alone was worth a wise man's book.

End o' the line, and lifting overhead,
  As in a graveyard costly shafts are wrought,
The House of Government, white to the sun,
  And in one room a fat man, doing naught.

Dana Burnet (1888–1962) was an American poet, journalist, and writer. He studied law at Cornell University, earning an LL.B. He did not, however, make his career in law practice. His first volume of poetry, in which "From an 'L' Train Window" was published, appeared in print in 1915.

From *Poems* by Dana Burnet. New York: Harper & Brothers Publishers, 1915.

* * * * *

This poem was enclosed in a letter to Andrew Johnston dated April 18, 1846. In the letter, Lincoln responds to a question in Johnston's prior letter as to whether Lincoln had authored a different poem, which Lincoln had apparently sent to Johnston as an enclosure to that letter. Lincoln indicated that he had not, but offered this poem which, he stated, was written after he returned to the neighborhood in Indiana where he grew up (and where his mother and sister were buried), after having been absent for fifteen years. As you read this poem, you might consider what domestic tranquility might have meant to this very private man who led a very public life.

~   Untitled

Abraham Lincoln

My childhood's home I see again,
    And sadden with the view;
And still, as memory crowds my brain,
    There's pleasure in it too.

O Memory! thou midway world
    'Twixt earth and paradise,
Where things decayed and loved ones lost
    In dreamy shadows rise,

And, freed from all that's earthly vile,
    Seem hallowed, pure and bright,
Like scenes in some enchanted isle
    All bathed in liquid light.

As dusky mountains please the eye
    When twilight chases day;
As bugle-notes that, passing by,
    In distance die away;

As leaving some grand waterfall,
    We, lingering, list its roar –
So memory will hallow all
    We've known but know no more.

Near twenty years have passed away
    Since here I bid farewell
To woods and fields, and scenes of play,
    And playmates loved so well.

Where many were, but few remain
    Of old familiar things;
But seeing them to mind again
    The lost and absent brings.

The friends I left that parting day,
>   How changed, as time has sped!
Young childhood grown, strong manhood gray;
>   And half of all are dead.

I hear the loved survivors tell
>   How nought from death could save,
Till every sound appears a knell,
>   And every spot a grave.

I range the fields with pensive tread,
>   And pace the hollow rooms,
And feel (companion of the dead)
>   I'm living in the tombs.

Abraham Lincoln (1809–1865) was the sixteenth president of the United States. He was born near Hodgenville, Kentucky, but the family moved to Perry County, Indiana in 1817 and again to Macon County, Illinois in 1830. Lincoln's mother died when he was nine years old, and his father's second wife encouraged his love of reading. Lincoln was a self-taught attorney and served in the Illinois General Assembly for eight years and the United States House of Representatives for one term before he became the Republican nominee for President in 1860. Although Lincoln's skills as an orator are well documented, he also both enjoyed poetry and wrote poetry from the time he was a teenager. The poem above is about the family's home in Perry County, Indiana.

From *Century Illustrated Monthly Magazine*, Volume 47 (1894).

✻   ✻   ✻   ✻

In his autobiography *A Long Way from Home*, McKay noted that the title of this poem was meant to be symbolic. This poem was first published in the May 1922 issue of the *Liberator* magazine, for which McKay worked at the time.

~ The White House

Claude McKay

Your door is shut against my tightened face,
And I am sharp as steel with discontent;
But I possess the courage and the grace
To bear my anger proudly and unbent.
The pavement slabs burn loose beneath my feet,
And passion rends my vitals as I pass,
A chafing savage, down the decent street,
Where boldly shines your shuttered door of glass.
Oh I must search for wisdom every hour,

Deep in my wrathful bosom sore and raw,
And find in it the superhuman power
To hold me to the letter of your law!
Oh, I must keep my heart inviolate,
Against the poison of your deadly hate!

Claude McKay (1889–1948) was a Jamaican writer and poet. McKay grew up in
Jamaica, leaving the island in 1912 to attend Booker T. Washington's Tuskegee
Institute, now Tuskegee University. In 1914, McKay moved to Harlem, where
he continued to publish his poetry and worked for *Liberator* magazine. Some of
his poetry was published under the pseudonym "Eli Edwards." After leaving the
United States for a period of travel, he returned to Harlem and published an autobiography entitled, *A Long Way from Home.* McKay is considered a key figure in
the Harlem Renaissance.

Reprinted in *Complete Poems* by Claude McKay, edited by William J. Maxwell.
Urbana: University of Illinois Press, 2004.

* * * * *

Subaltern, in its adjectival form, means lower in rank or position; subordinate.

～ **The Subalterns**

Thomas Hardy

I
"Poor wanderer," said the leaden sky,
     "I fain would lighten thee,
But there are laws in force on high
     Which say it must not be."

II
—"I would not freeze thee, shorn one," cried
     The North, "knew I but how
To warm my breath, to slack my stride;
     But I am ruled as thou."

III
—"To-morrow I attack thee, wight,"
     Said Sickness. "Yet I swear
I bear thy little ark no spite,
     But am bid enter there."

IV
—"Come hither, Son," I heard Death say;
     "I did not will a grave
Should end thy pilgrimage to-day,
     But I, too, am a slave!"

V

We smiled upon each other then,
 And life to me had less
Of that fell guise it wore ere when
 They owned their passiveness.

Thomas Hardy (1840–1928) was an English poet and novelist of the late Victorian and early modern era. He was so small at birth that he was at first believed to have been stillborn, and he stood only just over five feet tall as an adult. His father was a stonemason and a fiddler, and his musicality influenced Hardy's work, as did his mother's love of reading. In his youth, Hardy was apprenticed to an architect. The county of Dorset, where Hardy was born and raised, had considerable poverty; this difficult and rustic environment is reflected in Hardy's writings, which often explore themes of pain and human suffering. Although perhaps best known for the novels that brought him fame and financial security, Hardy wrote about a thousand poems, as well, and is said to have preferred his poetry to his prose.

From *The Collected Poems of Thomas Hardy*. London: MacMillan and Co., Limited, 1920.

* * * * *

The poem that appears below is the final poem in the collection entitled, *Flying Home through the Dark*, Judge Clarke's fifth collection of poems. In reading this poem, you might consider Judge Clarke's description of how poets use words, in which he quoted Lorna Crozier, also a Canadian poet: "For poets, words are windows for 'intense seeing.'"

~ **Going Home**

James Clarke

Be patient.
We are going home.
It is not far. We are rocking
in the great belly of the ship.
No light cracks the dark sea, but
the ship is strong, the voyage
will not be long.

We will arrive early.
It will be morning. We will
rub our unshelled eyes, see
the shore rise.
We will untangle our bones & play
in the lemon groves, dwell

in a white house near blue water.
There will be time. Be patient.
We are going home.

James Clarke was born in Peterborough, Ontario and educated at McGill University and Osgoode Hall. He practiced law in Cobourg, Ontario before being appointed to the bench in 1983. Now retired from the bench after many years of service as a superior court judge, Clarke resides in Guelph, Ontario. Judge Clarke's more than twenty books include numerous collections of poetry and three memoirs. In *The Kid from Simcoe Street: A Memoir and Poems*, Judge Clarke wrote about losing his beloved wife Mary to suicide and the way in which the poetry he began to write after her death rekindled his commitment as a judge as he redoubled his efforts to balance justice and mercy.

From *Flying Home Through the Dark* by James Clarke. Toronto: Exile Editions, Ltd., 2001.

∗   ∗   ∗   ∗   ∗

provide for the common defence

The United States Congress is commonly described as having "war powers," including the power to declare war and to provide appropriations for national defense. Congress has "peace powers," as well, including the power to approve international agreements and to appoint ambassadors, both of which help to resolve conflicts through diplomacy. Accordingly, this section explores themes of war and peace.

The section opens with "Who Made the Law," written through the eyes of a soldier serving on the front lines of one of the bloodiest battles in world history. It continues with "All Quiet Along the Potomac," a story of the death of a Civil War sentry that also introduces themes of class inequality. "Buttons" and "A Death-Bed" each, quite differently, invoke the human costs of war—"Buttons," through the flippancy of a "laughing young man," and "A Death-Bed," through the poet's anger as a father at the loss of his only son to war.

Perhaps the opposite of common defense is division and civil unrest. "Kent State, May 4, 1970," presents harrowing images of "kids . . . pouring lead into . . . other kids" as a country turns its military power on student demonstrators. "Freedom for the Mind" presents "common defense" in the sense of willingness to stand up for others' rights so that all are within the "common defense" being provided. This poem opens with images of high walls and iron gates as the poet finds himself in jail for protesting slavery, but closes with a reminder that chains may bind a person, but his mind will remain free.

In "I Will Stand Guard," the last poem in this section, the narrator is a sentry of a different sort, keeping watch for a loved one.

* * * * *

This poem, which was written in October 1916, was found in the possession of Leslie Coulson when he was killed at the age of 27. He died in the Battle of Le Transloy, the final offensive mounted by the British Fourth Army during the Battle of the Somme. With more than a million total casualties during the battle, which lasted from July through November 1916, the Battle of the Somme was one of the bloodiest in human history. The battle also showed the increasing importance of air power and marked the first use of the tank as a means of breaking the deadlock of the trench warfare that characterized World War I. As you read this poem, you might consider how it responds to the question posed in the title.

~   Who Made the Law?

Leslie Coulson

Who made the Law that men should die in meadows?
Who spake the word that blood should splash in lanes?
Who gave it forth that gardens should be bone-yards?
Who spread the hills with flesh, and blood, and brains?
                              Who made the Law?

Who made the Law that Death should stalk the village?
Who spake the word to kill among the sheaves,
Who gave it forth that death should lurk in hedgerows,
Who flung the dead among the fallen leaves?
                              Who made the Law?

Those who return shall find that peace endures,
Find old things old, and know the things they knew,
Walk in the garden, slumber by the fireside,
Share the peace of dawn, and dream amid the dew —
                              Those who return.

Those who return shall till the ancient pastures,
Clean-hearted men shall guide the plough-horse reins,
Some shall grow apples and flowers in the valleys,
Some shall go courting in summer down the lanes –
                              THOSE WHO RETURN.

But who made the Law? the Trees shall whisper to him:
"See, see the blood – the splashes on our bark!"
Walking the meadows, he shall hear bones crackle,
And fleshless mouths shall gibber in silent lanes at dark.
                              Who made the Law?

Who made the Law? At noon upon the hillside
His ears shall hear a moan, his cheeks shall feel a breath,
And all along the valleys, past gardens, croft and homesteads,
HE who made the Law,
                              He who made the Law,
He who made the Law shall walk along with Death.
                    WHO made the Law?

Trained as a journalist, Leslie Coulson (1889–1916) was an English war poet and a
sergeant with the 12th London Regiment—the Rangers. He served in World War I
and died on October 8, 1916, at the Somme from injuries sustained during the
Battle of Le Transloy on the Western Front. Coulson's poems were published posthumously in 1917, due to his father's efforts. His best known poem remains "Who
Made the Law?", written the month he died. A note below the poem as originally

published indicates a date of October 1916 and that the poem was found among Coulson's personal items when he died and was returned to his family with his other personal effects by the War Office.

From *From an Outpost and Other Poems* by Leslie Coulson. London: Harrison, Jehring & Co., Ltd., 1917.

✶ ✶ ✶ ✶ ✶

The title to this poem became a popular idiom meaning that nothing is happening. When the poem was published in 1861, the phrase would have been familiar to civilians and members of the military alike, as many of the dispatches from the Union Army during 1861 were entitled, "All Quiet Along the Potomac." As you read this poem, you might note the irony inherent in the title, and the way in which the title reinforces the class inequality that pervades the poem. The poem also had an immediate effect: its popularity resulted in both sides prohibiting the shooting of pickets.

～   **All Quiet Along the Potomac**

Ethyl Lynn Beers

"All quiet along the Potomac," they say,
    "Except, now and then, a stray picket
Is shot, as he walks on his beat to and fro,
    By a rifleman hid in the thicket.
'Tis nothing — a private or two now and then
    Will not count in the news of the battle;
Not an officer lost — only one of the men
    Moaning out, all alone, the death-rattle."

All quiet along the Potomac to-night,
    Where the soldiers lie peacefully dreaming;
Their tents, in the rays of the clear autumn moon
    Or the light of the watch-fire, are gleaming.
A tremulous sigh of the gentle night-wind
    Through the forest-leaves softly is creeping,
While stars up above, with their glittering eyes,
    Keep guard, for the army is sleeping.

There's only the sound of the lone sentry's tread
    As he tramps from the rock to the fountain,
And thinks of the two in the low trundle-bed,
    Far away in the cot on the mountain.
His musket falls slack; his face, dark and grim,
    Grows gentle with memories tender
As he mutters a prayer for the children asleep —
    For their mother; may Heaven defend her!

The moon seems to shine just as brightly as then,
    That night when the love yet unspoken
Leaped up to his lips —when low-murmured vows
    Were pledged to be ever unbroken.
Then, drawing his sleeve roughly over his eyes,
    He dashes off tears that are welling,
And gathers his gun closer up to its place,
    As if to keep down the heart-swelling.

He passes the fountain, the blasted pine tree,
    The footstep is lagging and weary;
Yet onward he goes through the broad belt of light,
    Toward the shade of the forest so dreary.
Hark! was it the night-wind that rustled the leaves?
    Was it moonlight so wondrously flashing?
It looked like a rifle — "Ha! Mary, good-bye!"
    The red life-blood is ebbing and plashing.

All quiet along the Potomac to-night,
    No sound save the rush of the river;
While soft falls the dew on the face of the dead—
    The picket's off duty for ever!

Born as Ethelinda Eliot, Ethel Lynn Beers (1827–1879) was a writer who focused on short stories and poems. "All Quiet Along the Potomac" is her best-known poem, originally titled "The Picket Guard" and published in *Harper's Weekly*, in the issue dated November 30, 1861.

From *All Quiet Along the Potomac and Other Poems* by Ethyl Lynn Beers. Philadelphia: Porter & Coates, 1879.

✶ ✶ ✶ ✶ ✶

The following poem was written at the height of World War I. The loss of life during World War I was greater than for any previous war in history, in part because of the new technologies of war such as tanks, machine guns, and poison gas.

~ Buttons

Carl Sandburg

I have been watching the war map slammed up for
    advertising in front of the newspaper office.
Buttons – red and yellow buttons – blue and black but-
    tons – are shoved back and forth across the map.

A laughing young man, sunny with freckles,
Climbs a ladder, yells a joke to somebody in the crowd,

And then fixes a yellow button one inch west
And follows the yellow button with a black button one
        inch west.

(Ten thousand men and boys twist on their bodies in
        a red soak along a river edge,
Gasping of wounds, calling for water, some rattling
        death in their throats.)
Who would guess what it cost to move two buttons one
        inch on the war map here in front of the newspaper
        office where the freckle-faced young man is laugh-
        ing to us?

Carl Sandburg (1878–1967) was an American poet, journalist, and biographer, and a three-time winner of the Pulitzer Prize. He won twice for his poetry, and once for his biography of Abraham Lincoln. Other than a brief stint at Lombard College, from which he did not graduate, Sandburg's formal education ended at age thirteen, when he went to work driving a milk wagon. He volunteered for duty during the Spanish-American war, where he was stationed in Puerto Rico. In 1965, Sandburg became the first white man to be honored with the NAACP's Silver Plaque Award, in recognition of his support for civil rights. The award, which also included lifetime membership in the NAACP, proclaimed Sandburg "a major prophet of civil rights in our time."

From *Chicago Poems* by Carl Sandburg. New York: Henry Holt and Company, 1916.

∗   ∗   ∗   ∗   ∗

This poem, published six months after the end of World War I, presents a fictionalized account of Kaiser Wilhelm II, the last German Emperor and King of Prussia, dying from throat cancer. It is generally considered one of Kipling's most savage poems, written out of grief and anger. Kipling's only son had died in the war in service to the British Army at the Battle of Loos. The choice of throat cancer is notable, as the Kipling family itself had a history of the disease. As you read this poem, note the three voices: the Kaiser, the physicians, and the commentator. "Regis suprema Voluntas lex," or "the highest law is the King's will," are the words that Kaiser Wilhelm II wrote in the City of Munich's Golden Book.

~   A Death-Bed

Rudyard Kipling

"This is the State above the Law.
        The State exists for the State alone."
*[This is a gland at the back of the jaw,
        And an answering lump by the collar-bone.]*

Some die shouting in gas or fire;
    Some die silent, by shell and shot.
Some die desperate, caught on the wire;
    Some die suddenly. This will not.

"Regis suprema Voluntas lex"
    [It will follow the regular course of—throats.]
Some die pinned by the broken decks,
    Some die sobbing between the boats.

Some die eloquent, pressed to death
    By the sliding trench, as their friends can hear.
Some die wholly in half a breath.
    Some—give trouble for half a year.

"There is neither Evil nor Good in life
    Except as the needs of the State ordain."
[Since it is rather too late for the knife,
    All we can do is to mask the pain.]

Some die saintly in faith and hope—
    One died thus in a prison-yard—
Some die broken by rape or the rope;
    Some die easily. This dies hard.

"I will dash to pieces who bar my way.
    Woe to the traitor! Woe to the weak!"
[Let him write what he wishes to say.
    It tires him out if he tries to speak.]

Some die quietly. Some abound
    In loud self-pity. Others spread
Bad morale through the cots around . . .
    This is a type that is better dead.

"The war was forced on me by my foes.
    All that I sought was the right to live."
[Don't be afraid of a triple dose;
    The pain will neutralize half we give.

Here are the needles. See that he dies
    While the effects of the drug endure. . . .
What is the question he asks with his eyes?—
    Yes, All-Highest, to God, be sure.]

Rudyard Kipling (1865–1936) was an English short-story writer, journalist, novelist, and poet. He was born in India and spent his first years there before being sent to England by his parents at age six. In 1882, he rejoined his family in India and began a career as a journalist, but then returned to England seven years later to pursue writing. He enjoyed some early success, married, and moved to Vermont in 1892. During his time in the United States before returning to England, he became a close acquaintance of Theodore Roosevelt. In 1907 he was one of the youngest recipients of the Nobel Prize in Literature. He was a war correspondent in South Africa during the Boer War and used his influence to secure for John, his only son, a position in the military during World War I after John had been rejected due to poor eyesight. Kipling had been a strong supporter of British involvement in the war. John, who was eighteen at the time of the Battle of Loos, was missing in action for two years before he was confirmed dead, and Kipling is said never to have fully recovered emotionally from the loss.

From *The Writings in Prose and Verse of Rudyard Kipling: The Years Between and Poems from History* by Rudyard Kipling. New York: Charles Scribner's Sons, 1919.

*   *   *   *   *

On May 4, 1970, Ohio National Guard troops opened fire on students at Kent State University. The students were protesting the military operations in Cambodia that President Nixon had announced a few days earlier. The student demonstration had begun on May 1, the day after President Nixon's announcement, and the crowd had grown to about 3,000 by May 4. The National Guardsmen initially used tear gas, and then shortly after noon, one fired his weapon. Ultimately, about 30 of the almost 80 guardsmen fired a total of about 70 rounds of ammunition, wounding nine and killing four.

~   Kent State, May 4, 1970

Paul Goodman

> Ran out of teargas and became panicky,
> inept kids, and therefore they poured lead
> into the other kids and shot them dead,
> and now myself and the whole country
> are weeping. It's not a matter of degree,
> not less not more than the Indo-Chinese slaughtered,
> it is the same. But folk are shattered
> by home truths – as I know who lost my boy.
>
> I am not willing to go on this week
> with business as usual, this month this year
> let cars slow down and stop and builders break
> off building and close up the theater.
> See, the children that we massacre
> are our own children. Call the soldiers back.

Paul Goodman (1911–1972) was a novelist, poet, and social critic. Goodman was born in New York City to a Jewish family that had emigrated from Germany. He was often labeled an anarchist, but he wrote extensively on a wide range of topics, including topics as disparate as city planning and psychoanalytic theory. Educated at the City University of New York, he taught at a variety of schools and was active in the war protests, draft resistance, and counterculture of the 1960s. He was bisexual and out, and his early activism for gay rights was part of the subject matter for the 2011 documentary film, *Paul Goodman Changed My Life*.

From *The Paul Goodman Reader*, edited by Taylor Stoehr. Oakland California: PM Press, 2011.

* * * * *

The following poem was said to have been written in 1835 while the poet was in jail for protesting slavery in the United States. This poem was reprinted many times, in many different publications. In the journal *Public Policy*, the poem was preceded by the following words: "The very name of Garrison brings liberty to our minds: his was a life-long devotion to the cause, whether working, writing, or singing, for chief among his poems are his odes to liberty."

~ **Freedom for the Mind**

William Lloyd Garrison

High walls and huge the body may confine,
    And iron gates obstruct the prisoner's gaze,
And massive bolts may baffle his design,
    And vigilant keepers watch his devious ways:
Yet scorns the immortal mind this base control!
    No chains can bind it, and no cell inclose:
Swifter than light, it flies from pole to pole,
    And, in a flash, from earth to heaven it goes!
It leaps from mount to mount – from vale to vale
    It wanders, plucking honeyed fruits and flowers;
It visits home, to hear the fireside tale,
    Or in sweet converse pass the joyous hours.
'Tis up before the sun, roaming afar,
    And, in its watches, wearies every star!

William Lloyd Garrison (1805–1879) was an American journalist and abolitionist, born in Newburyport, Massachusetts. He joined the abolitionist cause at age 25 and published a paper called *The Liberator* from 1831 to 1865. In the first issue of *The Liberator*, Garrison stated his views clearly: "I do not wish to think, or speak, or write, with moderation. . . . I am in earnest—I will not equivocate—I will not excuse—I will not retreat a single inch—AND I WILL BE HEARD." In addition to being a strong supporter of the abolitionist cause, Garrison supported temperance, free trade, and women's rights.

From *Public Policy*, Volume VIII. Chicago: Public Policy Publishing Co., 1903.

* * * * *

As you read this poem, you might note how the environment of Masters' sentry compares with that of Beers' sentry in "All Quiet Along the Potomac," and how these poems quite differently present the idea of common defense.

~ I Will Stand Guard

Edgar Lee Masters

I will stand guard
At the outpost of the stars,
In the darkness of deep midnights comet-scarred,
Where the burning worlds are ending with their wars.
In the blackness of eternity, the cold
Of the sunless spaces standing, I will wait.
I will wrap my cloak about me, be consoled
With the thought of your appearance soon or late.

When the sleeted flaw from planets long extinct
Blows about my spot of sentry slant and thin,
I shall smile upon my fancies interlinked,
I shall fold my arms and wait my hope to win.
If the flare of worlds that brighten and go out
Blind my watchfulness a moment, I will stand.
If dark shapes of vastness bellow in a rout,
While the wolf winds slink in terror, cry and whine,
Yet the undeserted post shall still be mine,
For it's then, perhaps, that I shall take your hand.

Oh, I had such love, such honor and such faith
All to give in life – to give them how I strove!
And it must be I shall give them after death,
When the sentryship is ended of my love,
When I find you. I shall find you if I keep
Still the lonely place for watching, if I wake
Heavy eyelids, all too weary, lest they sleep –
I will feed my hope with visions for your sake.
I will stand despite the blackness and the storm,
Gloved with hope and cloaked with wonder brave and warm.
For in life I was the watchman – then is what
Further watching and more waiting after earth
All is vanished down and ended and forgot?

What at last, if in my heart's despair and dearth
There's a stir of one approaching, as I planned;
And a voice at last that makes the silence starred?
You have found me and approved me – with your hand –
I will stand guard.

Edgar Lee Masters (1869–1950), was the author of *Spoon River Anthology* and a prominent American poet, dramatist, and lawyer. He was born in Garnett, Kansas, and grew up in and around Havana, Illinois, near Spoon River. Masters' father was also an attorney. Masters was active in the Democratic party and participated in William Jennings Bryan's presidential campaign. Masters' legal career was successful and varied, and included a period of law partnership with Clarence Darrow beginning in 1903, after which Masters opened his own firm in 1911.

From *Poetry: A Magazine of Verse*, edited by Harriet Monroe. Volume XXXII, Number III.

✷ ✷ ✷ ✷ ✷

promote the general Welfare

Professor Martha F. Davis has described the general welfare clause and its effect as follows, in her article "To Promote the General Welfare," published by the American Constitution Society in September 2011:

> *The national Constitution addresses economic and social rights prominently but with little specificity. The Preamble states that an overriding purpose of the U.S. Constitution is to "promote the general welfare," indicating that issues such as poverty, housing, food and other economic and social welfare issues facing the citizenry were of central concern to the framers. However, the Bill of Rights has been largely construed to provide procedural mechanisms for fair adjudication of those rights rather than carving out claims on the government to ensure that individuals actually have any social and economic assets to protect.*

The first poems in this section demonstrate the need for meaningful concern for the general welfare in the context of homelessness, prison conditions, and the bankruptcy system, in "Grant Park," "To the Unknown Dutch Postcard-Sender (1988)," and "Bankruptcy Hearing," respectively. The poems that follow, "Kin-jeh's song about the abstemious Chancellor," "Prisoners of the Tower," "The Golf Links Lie So Near the Mill," and "Breathless," illustrate the lip service that is sometimes given to general welfare, using examples drawn from poverty, juvenile justice, child labor, and disability rights.

⁕ ⁕ ⁕ ⁕ ⁕

This poem was first published in *The Messenger* magazine in March 1924. *The Messenger* was published in Harlem from 1917 to 1928 and was an important part of the Harlem Renaissance. In the poem below, it is believed that the poet is referring to New York City's Bryant Park, which is adjacent to the New York Public Library and is sometimes described as Manhattan's Town Square. On any given night in the United States, more than half a million people experience homelessness.

~ Grant Park

Langston Hughes

The haunting face of poverty,
The hands of pain,
The rough, gargantuan feet of fate,

The nails of conscience in a soul
That didn't want to do wrong –
You can see what they've done
To brothers of mine
In one back-yard of Fifth Avenue.
You can see what they've done
To brothers of mine –
Sleepers on iron benches
Behind the Library in Grant Park.

Langston Hughes (1902–1967) was an influential poet and writer, often considered a founder of the cultural movement known as the Harlem Renaissance. Hughes gained acclaim for his highly experimental use of rhyme and dialect and for his realistic portrayal of the lives of many African Americans in urban areas. Hughes remained a prolific writer for the span of four decades while also travelling extensively in Mexico, France, Italy, Spain, West Africa and the Soviet Union. His works not only discuss prevalent racial issues of the United States, but also explore the displacement and alienation that typified much of Hughes' experience of law.

Reprinted in *The Collected Poems of Langston Hughes*, edited by Arnold Rampersad & David Roessel. New York: Random House, 1994.

✳   ✳   ✳   ✳   ✳

Jack Mapanje was detained in Mikuyu Maximum Security Prison in Malawi for three years, seven months, sixteen days, and about twelve hours with no charges being brought against him. Even upon his release, he was never informed as to what crime he had ostensibly committed, although he has indicated he expects it had to do with certain of his poems in the book *Of Chameleons and Gods*, which was said to be a subversive critique of H.K. Banda's dictatorship in Malawi. In an account from the book *The Word Behind Bars and the Paradox of Exile* edited by Kofi Anyidoho, Mapanje makes it clear that the poem commemorates a real event and that the postcard brought greetings from someone whose signature he could not—and was not meant to—decipher. The distance from the Hague, Netherlands to Zomba, Malawi is more than 7,300 miles. As you read the poem, you might consider why the postcard sent "waves of hope and reason" through the cell block.

~   To the Unknown Dutch Postcard-Sender (1988)

Jack Mapanje

I.

Your *Groeten uit Holland* postcard, with
Five pictures, dear unknown fighter for
My freedom, should not have arrived here
Really; first, your shameless address:

There are too many villages 'NEAR ZOMBA,
MALAWI', for anything to even stray into
Mikuyu Prison; then, I hear, with those
Bags upon bags of protest letters, papers,
Books, literary magazines, postcards,
Telexes, faxes and what not, received at
Central Sorting Office Limbe Post Office
Everyday, later dispatched to my Headmaster
And his henchpersons and the Special
Branch and their informers to burn, file
Or merely sneer at and drop in dustbins –
Your postcard had no business reaching
Mikuyu Prison. And how did you guess I
Would eventually sign my Detention Order
(No 264), October 21, and I desperately
Desired some other solidarity signature
To stand by (to give me courage and cheer)
However Dutch, however enigmatic, stamped
Roosendaal, posted Den Haag, 23 October
1988, to buttress this shattered spirit
And these mottled bare feet squelching
On this sodden life-sucking rough cement
Of Mikuyu Prison ground? But many thanks,
Many thanks on behalf of these D4s too!

II.

You send me those Dutch tourist colours
I'd probably have spurned outside, but
In these soggy red-brick and cracking
Cement walls, a sun-burnt Dutch *clogger*
In black cap, blue shirt, orange apron,
Chocolate trousers and brown wooden shoes
Selling white, red, and yellow clogs,
Beside a basketful of more white clogs,
Is a spectacle too tantalizing for these
Badly holed Levi's shoes and blistered
Feet! You offer me Dutch men folk in
White trousers and white shirts and red,
Blue and yellow hats declaring heaps on
Heaps of Edam cheeses on oval-shaped
Pine trays buoyantly shaming our ghoulish
Goulash of gangrenous cow bones mashed
In rabid weevil-ridden red kidney beans!
You proffer Dutch bell-shaped houses
Beside fruit trees, a family strolling along
The avenue—this concrete church with
Arches and Corinthian columns probably

Beat the bombs. A Dutch mother and daughter
In white folk-hats and black and white
Pretty frocks sitting on trimmed green
Lawn, offer each other red tulips beside
A colony of yellow tulips. And I present
You these malaria infested and graffiti
Bespattered walls, without doctors, priests
And twelve months of barred visits from
Wife, daughters, son, relatives, friends!

III.

But, however these colours slipped through
Our post office sorters, your *Groeten uit Holland*
My dear, has sent waves of hope and reason
To hang-on to the fetish walls of these
Cold cells. Today, the midnight centipedes
Shriller than howling hyenas will dissolve;
We will not feel those rats nibbling at
The rotting cones of our toes. And that
Midnight piss from the blotched lizards
Won't stink; and if the scorpion stings
Again tonight, the stampede in D4 will jump
In jubilation of our *Groeten uit Holland!*

Jack Mapanje (b. 1944) is a Malawi poet, as well as a linguist, editor, and human rights activist. He is the author of six collections of poetry. After the publication of his first book of poetry, *Of Chameleons and Gods*, he was imprisoned for what the Malawi government considered subversive poetry. He spent three years, seven months, and sixteen days as a political prisoner before his release and now lives in York, with his family, in exile. Among his honors include the 1988 Rotterdam Poetry International Award for *Of Chameleons and Gods* and the African Literature Association's Fonlon-Nichols Award for literary excellence and a commitment to human rights.

From *The Last of the Sweet Bananas: New and Selected Poems* by Jack Mapanje. Tarset: Bloodaxe Books, Ltd., 2004.

* * * * *

The word "bankrupt" comes from the Italian "banca rotta," or "broken bench." When an artisan was unable to pay his debts, his bench was broken, both as a mark of shame and to prevent him from continuing in business. As you read this poem, you might consider how its use of analogies to livestock, children in school, and parishioners in a church—and how the poet's artful use of punctuation—affect the experience of reading the poem.

~   Bankruptcy Hearing

Dana Bisignani

They have us corralled
in the basement of the courthouse.
One desk and a row of folding chairs—
just like first grade, our desks facing Teacher
in neat little rows.

        Upstairs,
wooden benches like pews and red
carpet reserved for those who've held out
the longest. No creditors have come to claim us
today. We're small-time.

This guy from the graveyard shift
stares at his steel-toed boots, nervous hands
in his lap. None of us look each other
in the eye. We steal quick looks—*how did you
get here*. . .

chemo bills, a gambling addiction,
a summer spent unemployed and too many
cash advances to pay the rent.
We examine the pipes that hang
from the ceiling, the scratched tiles on the floor,

the red glow of the exit sign at the end of the hall
so like our other failed escapes:
light of the TV at night,
glass of cheap Merlot beside a lamp,
a stop light on the way out of town.

Dana Bisignani holds an M.F.A. in poetry from Purdue University, and both an M.A. and a B.A. in English from Western Illinois University. Her poetry has appeared in journals such as *Cimarron Review, Prairie Schooner,* and *Poetry East.* She grew up on Chicago's South Side and has lived and taught creative writing and women's studies throughout the Midwest. She is a community organizer and educator currently living in Fargo, ND.

Published in *Blue Collar Review,* Vol. 12, Issue 2, Winter 2008–2009.

✶ ✶ ✶ ✶ ✶

This poem seems to refer to Sir Stafford Cripps, Chancellor of the Exchequer, who was known for his austerity. An April 18, 1949, article in *Time Magazine* entitled "The Iron Chancellor" referred to him as "the abstemious chancellor." In the 1930s, biographer John Fuegi indicates, Brecht adopted a poetic persona he called "Kin-Jeh," modeled on fifth-century Confucian philosopher Me-Ti. This poem was originally published as part of a body of aphorisms Brecht wrote in this persona.

~ Kin-jeh's song about the abstemious Chancellor

Bertolt Brecht

I have heard it said, the Chancellor doesn't drink
He eats no meat and doesn't smoke
And he lives in a small apartment.
But I have also heard it said that the poor
Are starving and prostrated in misery.
How much better would a state be of which one could say:
The Chancellor lolls drunkenly in the cabinet
Contemplating the smoke from their pipes, a handful
Of ignoramuses doctor the statutes
There are no poor people.

Bertolt Brecht (1898–1956) was a German poet, theatre director, and playwright. He served as a medical orderly during World War I and was deeply moved by the scenes he witnessed. In 1933, after the Reichstag fire, Brecht fled Germany, which ultimately removed his citizenship, rendering him a stateless citizen. He sought asylum in Sweden and Finland, and moved to the United States in 1941, where he remained until 1947, at which time his plays and poems and connections with Marxism resulted in a hearing before the House Committee on Un-American Activities. During the hearing, Brecht adamantly defended the free exchange of ideas and his own viewpoints. In response to a question regarding his "revolutionary" writings, Brecht famously stated, "I have written a number of poems and songs and plays in the fight against Hitler, and of course they can be considered therefore as revolutionary, 'cause I of course was for the overthrow of that government." Brecht also injected some humor into the proceedings: when Robert Stripling, as Chief Investigator, read an English translation of Brecht's "Forward, We've Not Forgotten," and asked whether he had written it, Brecht responded, "No, I wrote a German poem, but that is very different." Shortly after the hearing, Brecht left for East Germany, where he continued to write and died of a heart attack in 1956.

From *The Collected Poems of Bertolt Brecht* by Bertolt Brecht, translated by David Constantine and Tom Kuhn. New York: Liveright Publishing Company, 2018.

✳   ✳   ✳   ✳   ✳

From the *Committee on Child Abuse Investigation Committee Report Vol. I, Chapter 15: St. Conleth's Reformatory School, Daingean, County Offaly, 1940–1973:*

15.110: In the light of the evidence heard, it is clear that floggings were . . . administered for many . . . misbehaviours. It was also clear that the way in which staff interpreted what amounted to insubordination or deliberate destruction of property was so wide, that minor offences and even accidents could result in the most severe punishment.

As a young man, the poet was sent to the industrial school in Daingean, Ireland, described in the opening quote.

~ Prisoners of the Tower

Patrick Galvin

I can see them now
Prisoners of the tower
Their faces blind
From centuries of barbed-wire.

If you are guilty
You know you are guilty
If you are innocent
You would not be here.

You are here
Therefore . . .

1

When the cell door closes
Behind you
You are free
When the cell door closes
Behind you
You are free
When the cell door closes
Behind you
You are free to weep
Endlessly
Without tears.

It is an offence
To shed tears in the tower
It is an offence
To grow old in the tower
It is an offence
To sit in the tower
But
You may walk freely
From wall to wall

And contemplate
The absence of bread.

Under our system of Government
A man has these rights:
You may walk freely from wall to wall
And contemplate the absence of bread.

2

You may not
Hear voices.

All prisoners
Who hear voices
Will report such voices
To the Keeper of the tower.
These voices do not exist
And if they do exist
They will be shot.
The shooting of voices
Is essential
To the harmony
Of the tower.

All prisoners
Who fail to report
The hearing of voices
Will be shot.
All prisoners
Who report the hearing of voices
Will be sent to a lunatic asylum.
Prisoners who are sent to a lunatic asylum
May
Lose the freedom of the tower
But the voices will stop.

Under our system of Government
A man has these rights:
You may lose the freedom of the tower
But the voices will stop.

3

You are free
To die.

All prisoners
Are entitled to death

All prisoners
Are entitled to a speedy death.
Any prisoner
Who is not capable of committing suicide
Will be shot
Any prisoner
Who fails to report
A desire to commit suicide
Will be shot.

When a prisoner dies in his cell
His body will remain in his cell.
It is an offence
To remove the dead from their cells.
It is assumed that in due time
Nature will corrupt the flesh
But the bones
If any
Remain the sole property of the prisoner.
He may return for these bones
At any time.

Under our system of Government
The dead also have rights:
You may return for these bones
At any time.

You are free
To have them.

Patrick Galvin (1927–2011) was born in Cork and was an Irish poet, songwriter, and playwright. The three years he spent as a young boy at St. Conleth's Industrial School after having been called "disruptive" were harrowing and brutal, and he became a life-long advocate for the oppressed. Galvin was among the first to speak out about the abuse that he and others experienced, long before the publication of the report that is cited in the introduction to this poem. During World War II, he joined the Royal Air Force, although he was actually underage at the time. Galvin served tours of duty in the United Kingdom, the Middle East, and Africa. He began writing poetry in about 1950 and published his first volume of poetry, *Heart of Grace*, in 1957. Galvin traveled extensively in the 1950s, 60s, and 70s, spending periods of time in London, Dublin, Spain, Belfast, and rural Ireland. A prolific writer whose zeal for life was not slowed by a stroke that left him wheel-chair-bound for the last several years of his life, he is considered one of the leading Irish poets and dramatists of his generation.

From *New and Selected Poems* by Patrick Galvin. Cork: Cork University Press, 1996.

* * * * *

In 1900, almost twenty percent of American workers were less than sixteen years old. Efforts to regulate or eliminate child labor faced considerable opposition at both the state and federal level, with the Supreme Court declaring federal child labor laws unconstitutional in 1916 and 1918, during the period in which the poem below was published. The Great Depression created a strong incentive to remove children from the workforce, and the Fair Labor Standards Act of 1938 placed limitations on child labor, including restricting the hours that children may work and barring the employment of children entirely in certain fields.

~ The Golf Links Lie So Near the Mill

Sarah N. Cleghorn

The golf links lie so near the mill
    That almost every day
The laboring children can look out
    And see the men at play.

Sarah Norcliffe Cleghorn (1876–1959) was born in Norfolk, Virginia. She was a teacher, poet, and reformer. She earned a bachelor's degree in literature and philosophy from Radcliffe College and contributed short stories and poems to many of the leading magazines of her time. She was involved in women's suffrage, civil rights, prison reform, and labor reform, especially with respect to child labor. The poem above, which is considered her most famous, comes from Cleghorn's first published collection of poetry. It is actually a quatrain from a longer poem, "In the Needle's Eye."

From *Portraits and Protests* by Sarah N. Cleghorn. New York: Henry Holt and Company, 1917.

* * * * *

In a September 2019 interview that is part of the Wombwell Rainbow series, Lightbown shared the experience of writing one of his early poems, a letter poem. He chose to write to his legs. In a quote from that interview, Lightbown stated, "I don't know why and it was the first time I had written about my spinal injury and my relationship with my body. From that moment I couldn't stop and here I am six years later with my first collection just published and many book shelves stacked with poetry." The full interview is available at https://thewombwellrainbow.com/2019/09/01/wombwell-rainbow-interviews-stephen-lightbown/.

~ Breathless

Stephen Lightbown

It started. A typed question–
Do you have wheelchair access?

Grew. A one sentence reply –
Yes, can they manage one step?
They. I did not correct.
Prised free from my paralysis,
put it to one side
with yesterday's labels.
Replaced cared for sympathy
with credit for caring.
Deceit: I had trusted myself.
Jumped,
the first chance I got.
The ground suddenly sturdy under
feet. Who is this man that stands
inside of me?
I enquire with Mozart fingers.
Feel tendons hatch from hibernation.
Feel denim against legs.
Feel thighs swell with years
of walking.
I'm out of control –
Do you . . . ? Three restaurants,
a theatre, two hotels,
gin tasting. I guess I drink now too.
Out of breath from untruths.
Weightless with new footsteps.
Stop pushing.
Ask me, ask me,
What do they need?
We'll be fine,
     we are
         quite
            independent.
               Quite.

Stephen Lightbown was born in 1979 in Blackburn, Lancashire, England. He was paralyzed in 1996 at age sixteen from a sledging accident, and he uses a wheelchair as a result. He is a novelist, poet, and champion for individuals experiencing disability. Much of his poetry focuses on his experiences as a wheelchair user, although he writes about other subjects as well. Lightbown offers workshops that focus on disability poetry, as well as issues of access and how poets write about their relationships with their bodies. He currently has two volumes of poetry, *Only Air* and *The Last Custodian*.

From *We Are Not Your Metaphor: A Disability Poetry Anthology*, edited by Zoeglossia Fellows. Minneapolis: Squares & Rebels, 2019.

✳ ✳ ✳ ✳ ✳

Secure the Blessings of Liberty

The legal profession is intended to be self-regulating. The following language from the commentary to the American Bar Association's Model Rules of Professional Conduct provides a glimpse into the standards to which attorneys are expected to hold themselves:

> *Self-regulation of the legal profession requires that members of the profession initiate disciplinary investigation when they know of a violation of the Rules of Professional Conduct. Lawyers have a similar obligation with respect to judicial misconduct. An apparently isolated violation may indicate a pattern of misconduct that only a disciplinary investigation can uncover. Reporting a violation is especially important where the victim is unlikely to discover the offense.*

From American Bar Association Model Rules of Professional Conduct, Rule 8.3, Comment 1. This language appears in a section entitled, "Maintaining the Integrity of the Profession." As you read the poems that follow, you might consider the relationship between self-rule and liberty.

The first four poems present various perspectives on liberty. In Emerson's untitled poem that opens this section, liberty is self-reliance. In Dickenson's untitled poem that follows, liberty could be freedom from rules. Gilman presents liberty as truth, courage, love, and work. In Wheatley's poem, liberty is freedom. These poems are followed by three that illustrate some challenges to liberty. In Untermeyer's poem, the law, while powerful, is sterile and remote. In Millay's, the challenge to liberty is a lack of central motivating purpose. In Rajendra's, constitutional liberties have been eliminated.

✳ ✳ ✳ ✳ ✳

In *Self-Reliance and Other Essays*, Emerson stated, "What I must do, is all that concerns me, not what the people think." This perspective pervades the poem that follows.

~ Untitled

Ralph Waldo Emerson

I will not live out of me
I will not see with others' eyes

My good is good, my evil ill
I would be free – I cannot be
While I take things as others please to rate them
I dare attempt to lay out my own road
That which myself delights in shall be Good
That which I do not want, – indifferent,
That which I hate is Bad. That's flat
Henceforth, please God, forever I forego
The yoke of men's opinions. I will be
Lighthearted as a bird & live with God.
I find him in the bottom of my heart
I hear continually his Voice therein
And books, & priests, & worlds, I less esteem
Who says the heart's a blind guide? It is not.
My heart did never counsel me to sin
I wonder where it got its wisdom
For in the darkest maze amid the sweetest baits
Or amid horrid dangers never once
Did that gentle Angel fail of his oracle
The little needle always knows the north
The little bird remembereth his note
And this wise Seer never errs
I never taught it what it teaches me
I only follow when I act aright.
Whence then did this Omniscient Spirit come?
From God it came. It is the Deity.

Ralph Waldo Emerson (1803–1882) was a major American poet and a leader in the Transcendentalist movement. He was born in Boston and began writing poetry at the age of nine. The poem above is part of a manuscript of poems from 1830 through 1839. Emerson's poetry tends to reflect highly romanticized views of individualism, his fixation on the divinity of nature, and his reliance on intuition as a model for understanding the universe.

From *Emerson: Collected Poems and Translations*. New York: The Library of America, 1994.

* * * * *

These lines are taken from an undated letter to Mrs. Edward Tuckerman. Dickinson had enclosed some rich caramels she had prepared, the recipe for which her friend had apparently requested. The lines below are from her response indicating no recipe exists.

~ Untitled

Emily Dickinson

We have no statutes here,
but each does as it will,
which is the sweetest
jurisprudence.

Emily Dickinson (1830–1886) was an American poet, born in Amherst, Massachusetts. Her grandfather founded Amherst College, and her father was an attorney in addition to serving as a state legislator. Although Dickinson was an excellent and engaged student, her formal education ended at age 18. She wrote prolifically, also maintaining robust correspondence with a number of contacts. Although Dickinson wrote nearly 2,000 poems, most of her work remained unpublished until after her death, and the first publications edited and altered her work considerably. Thomas H. Johnson's 1955 *Complete Poems* is generally considered to be the first posthumous publication of Dickinson's poetry that was true to its intended form and content.

From *The Life and Letters of Emily Dickinson* by Martha Dickinson Bianchi. New York: Houghton Mifflin Company, 1924.

* * * * *

The poem below was published in *The Forerunner*, which was a monthly magazine that Gilman herself wrote, edited, owned, and published. On the front page of the magazine appear these words: "[*The Forerunner*] stands for Humanness in Women, and in Men; for better methods in Child-culture; for the Home that is no Workshop; for the New Ethics, the New Economics, the New World we are to make—are making."

~ The Human Law

Charlotte Perkins Gilman

We watch the solemn courses of the stars,
And feel the swell of reverence and praise.
Even though some may fall: . . .

    We watch the birds,
The small birds, finding each her food and mate;
Nest-building, happy, busy, free from care,
Even though some may starve: . . .

    We see in these
The smooth fulfillment of their nature's law;
They are content and calm and good to see,

Because of this fulfillment; they are true.
And we? Have we no law? May we not show
That power in peace, that happiness in work,
That rich contentment in our share of life,—
Even though some may fail? . . .
　　　　What is our law?

Truth: To be true: To hold oneself in line
With the uplifting forces of the world,
That lift us as they lifted continents;
　　　Truth to one's work.

Courage: The courage that can stand alone
Against the doubt and hate of millions here,
Against the million millions of the past,
Against one's own distrust.
　　　Courage that stands.

Love: To wish well to all the human race;
To will toward happiness for every one.
To feel, to guard, to give—
　　　Love actual.

Work: Not pay-earning, but the outflow wide
Of one's best powers in special services,
Those subtle services that build the world,
Each for the others, organized and strong.
This is the Human Law. So we should live,
Each honestly fulfilling one's own task,
In love and courage; seeing in that work
The smooth fulfillment of our nature's law,
　　　Even though some may fail. . . .

Charlotte Perkins Gilman (1860–1935) was an American poet, writer, and social activist. During her first marriage, Gilman suffered a severe episode of post-partum depression that would form the impetus for her short story *The Yellow Wallpaper*, which is the best-selling book of all time for The Feminist Press at the City University of New York. Following her separation and divorce from her first husband, Gilman began to advocate for suffrage and women's rights, joining a number of public causes on behalf of women's rights. She also met and married her second husband, a Wall Street lawyer. Suffering from incurable breast cancer, shortly after her second husband died, Gilman committed suicide in 1935, stating that she "chose chloroform over cancer."

From *The Forerunner* by Charlotte Perkins Gilman. Vol. 3, No. 1, January 1912.

✳　✳　✳　✳　✳

William Legge, Second Earl of Dartmouth, was appointed His Majesty's Principal Secretary of State for the Colonies in 1772. The poet was hopeful that his appointment would result in the abolition of slavery in the colonies, as she knew that several of his close friends and acquaintances were abolitionists. The poem that follows was published in 1773 and expresses her hope.

~ To the Right Honorable William, Earl of Dartmouth, His Majesty's Principal Secretary of State for North America, etc.

Phillis Wheatley

Hail, happy day, when smiling like the morn,
Fair *Freedom* rose New England to adorn;
The northern clime beneath her genial ray,
Dartmouth congratulates thy blissful sway;
Elate with hope her race no longer mourns,
Each soul expands, each grateful bosom burns,
While in thine hand with pleasure we behold
The silken reins, and Freedom's charms unfold.
Long lost to realms beneath the northern skies
She shines supreme, while hated faction dies;
Soon as appeared the *Goddess* long desir'd,
Sick at the view, she languish'd and expir'd;
Thus from the splendors of the morning light
The owl in sadness seeks the caves of night.

No more *America,* in mournful strain
Of wrongs, and grievance unredress'd complain,
No longer shall thou dread the iron chain,
Which wanton *Tyranny* with lawless hand
Had made, and with it meant to enslave the land.
Should you, my lord, while you peruse my song,
Wonder from whence my love of *Freedom* sprung,
Whence flow these wishes for the common good,
By feeling hearts alone best understood,
I, young in life, by seeming cruel fate
Was snatch'd from Afric's fancy'd happy seat;
What pangs excruciatingly must molest,
What sorrows labour in my parent's breast?
Steel'd was that soul and by no misery mov'd
That from a father seized his babe belov'd;
Such, such my case. And can I then but pray
Others may never feel tyrannic sway?

For favors past, great Sir, our thanks are due,
And thee we ask thy favors to renew,

Since in thy pow'r, as in thy will before,
To sooth the griefs, which thou didst once deplore.
May heav'nly grace the sacred sanction give
To all thy works, and thou forever live
Not only on the wings of fleeting *Fame*,
Though praise immortal crowns the patriot's name,
But to conduct to heav'n's refulgent fane,
May fiery coursers sweep th' ethereal plain,
And bear thee upwards to the blest abode,
Where, like the prophet, thou shalt find thy God.

Phillis Wheatley (1753–1784) was an African slave, taken from Senegal / Gambia, West Africa, when she was about seven years old—an experience she referenced in her poems. Wheatley, who was taught how to read and write by the family who purchased and eventually manumitted her, became a published poet with almost thirty poems before she was eighteen. The collection was published in London because no publisher in the colonies was willing to publish her work. Wheatley is believed to have written many more poems than have been published or discovered. She is widely credited as having been the first African-American poet to have a book of poems published under her own name. A strong supporter of American independence, she sent one of her poems in honor of George Washington to him. Later, at his invitation, Wheatley visited his headquarters in Cambridge, Massachusetts in 1776.

From *Poems on Various Subjects, Religious and Moral*, Phillis Wheatley. London: Archibald Bell, 1773.

* * * * *

The word "cant" in the following poem most likely refers to the use of language, whether it be jargon or chant.

~   Portrait of a Supreme Court Judge

Louis Untermeyer

How well this figure represents the Law—
    This pose of neuter justice, sterile cant;
This Roman Emperor with the iron jaw,
    Wrapped in the black silk of a maiden-aunt.

Louis Untermeyer (1885–1977) was an American poet, anthologist, author, and translator. His father was a jeweler. For a time, he worked with his father in the jewelry business, having left high school to do so, before leaving the business to pursue writing as a full-time career. Robert Frost, Ezra Pound, and Arthur Miller were part of his circle of acquaintances. He was married a total of five times to four different women and was, over his lifetime, the author or editor of almost one hundred books. He won the Poetry Society of America's Gold Medal in 1956 and was also the Consultant in Poetry to the Library of Congress from 1961 to 1963.

From *These Times* by Louis Untermeyer. London: Henry Holt & Co., 1917.

✶   ✶   ✶   ✶   ✶

The volume in which this poem appears opens with the following words from Max Eastman, who edited *The Masses* magazine: "It takes very few individuals to make a new age or explode an old one. That is, if the individuals themselves have hold of a vital substance." As you read this poem, you might consider what "vital substance" would prevent an America that is "Beautiful Nowhere."

~   To the Liberty Bell

Edna St. Vincent Millay

Toll, toll,
O cracked and venerable!
Start swinging suddenly
And speak
Upon this jigging air.

Tell us of a day when men stood up in meeting
And spoke of God,
And nobody laughed.

Toll, toll.

They say we have no leader now. It may be.
I know
We have no cause.

America!—Beautiful Nowhere in the hearts of a few
Periwigged men
Sitting about a table.

Toll, toll.

Yet toll not.
Lest to our shame we learn how few to-day
Would stand in the street and listen.
Only some lean, half-hearted anarchist
Who happened to be out;
And the children,
That shout at air-planes.

Edna St. Vincent Millay (1892–1950) was both a poet and a dramatist. She was raised by her mother, a nurse, from the age of eight, and Millay spoke warmly of her mother's support and encouragement. It was her mother who encouraged her, at the age of twenty, to participate in the poetry contest sponsored by *The Lyric Year* that ultimately brought her to public notice, even though her poem did not win the contest. In 1923, she won the Pulitzer Prize in poetry – the first woman to do so. She also won the Poetry Society of America's Robert Frost Medal for distinguished lifetime achievement in American poetry, in 1943.

From *May Days: An Anthology of Verse from Masses-Liberator*, edited by Genevieve Taggard. New York: Boni & Liveright, Inc., 1925.

＊　＊　＊　＊　＊

The poem below was reprinted in the June 1984 issue of the International Commission of Jurists' journal *The Review*. The ICJ is a non-governmental organization, founded in 1952 in Geneva, which is focused on international human rights. Mr. Rajendra's poem followed updates on human rights throughout the world, from East Timor, to Haiti, to Japan, Pakistan, South Africa, and Western Sahara. As you read this poem, you might consider the world-wide applicability of its themes.

~   The Dark Side of Trees

Cecil Rajendra

The truth burns
so they turned
their faces away
from the sun . . .

When small liberties
    began to fray . . .
When their constitution
    was being chipped away
When their newspapers
    were shut down . . .
When their rule of law
    was twisted round . . .
When might became right
    and their friends
Were carried off screaming
    in the pitch of night . . .

They chose silence
feigned blindness
pleaded ignorance.

And now when the shadow
    of the jackboot hangs
ominous over their beloved land
    they walk as zombies
unable to distinguish right from
    wrong from right
their minds furred with lichens
    like the dark side of trees.

    The truth burns
    so they turned
    their faces away
    from the sun . . .

Cecil Rajendra is a poet, lawyer, and human rights activist who has lived by the mantra, "Seek out the little guy and help if you can." He was born in 1941 in Penang, Malaysia and received his formal education at St. Xavier's Institution, the University of Singapore and Lincoln's Inn (London) where he qualified as a barrister-at-law. Throughout his lengthy and distinguished career, he has earned numerous distinctions in poetry, law, and human rights. As an attorney, in 1980 he co-founded the Penang Legal Aid Centre (PLAC), which was the first rural legal aid clinic in Malaysia. In 2000, he created Malaysia's first-ever mobile legal aid clinic. For this work, Rajendra earned the Malaysian Bar's 2019 Lifetime Achievement Award as well as the International Bar Association's 2019 Pro Bono Award. As a poet, he has published dozens of volumes of poetry and was nominated for the 2004 Nobel Prize in Literature for his collection *By Trial & Terror*. His work has been published in more than fifty countries and translated into a number of languages. As a human rights activist, he has initiated campaigns against detention without trial and in support of an independent judiciary. He was awarded the first-ever Malaysian Lifetime Humanitarian Award in 2004, in recognition of both his outstanding work in law and his exemplary poetry; and in 2015 was declared a Living Heritage Treasure by the Penang Heritage Trust.

From *Hour of Assassins and Other Poems* by Cecil Rajendra. London: Bogle-L'Ouverture Publications, 1982.

* * * * *

Choose ADA Rules of Professional Conduct: Pick a rule that just makes sense to me.

On Tuesday: writing a complaint

to ourselves and our Posterity

This closing section of the anthology looks to the future, examining the world the next generations will inherit. The MacNeice poem serves to illuminate the risk of empty consumerism. Melville's explores both the "midnight" of war and the "morn" of peace. The poems that follow invite the reader into a place of hope and anticipation. Luke speaks of beauty, hope, and abundance. Zolynas reminds us of our interconnectedness with one another. Tagore's poem speaks of truth, freedom, reason, and purpose. Press shows us the vastness of our world, in which, though we are but "coal dust" in the "big, black nowhere of the universe," we can be part of something radiant and beautiful. And finally, in the words of her beautiful poem inscribed on the Statue of Liberty, Lazarus shows us a shining vision of these United States: A "world-wide welcome" from a "mighty woman with a torch" who stands "beside the golden door."

✶ ✶ ✶ ✶

The poem from which the lines below were taken, "As in Their Time," consists of 12 numbered 5-line stanzas, each of which can be read individually and which were also arranged as a choral composition for a chamber choir. As you read this poem, you might consider the implications of "liv[ing] among plastic gear," as reflected in this poem, and how this could affect a person's experience of being alive. In addition, you might consider how the universe is "ever-expanding" even in ways that the poet may not have been able to envision when the poem was written.

~ *From* As in Their Time

Louis MacNeice

(x)

Citizen of an ever-expanding
Universe, burning smokeless fuel,
He had lived among plastic gear so long
When they decided to fingerprint him
He left no fingerprints at all.

Louis MacNeice (1907–1963) was an Irish poet and playwright prominent in the 1930s. He was born in Belfast and began writing poetry at age seven. While a student at Oxford majoring in classics and philosophy, MacNeice befriended the poets W.H. Auden, Stephen Spender, and Cecil Day-Lewis. Later in life, MacNeice worked for the BBC, and he was awarded the CBE in 1958. MacNeice's "As in Their Time" was part of his final collection of poetry, *The Burning Perch*. The volume was published a few days following MacNeice's unexpected death at age 55.

From *The Burning Perch* by Louis MacNeice. London: Faber & Faber, 1963.

＊　＊　＊　＊　＊

During the Civil War, the Northern Lights were visible as far south as Virginia. During the Battle of Fredericksburg, some observers described the sky as "red as blood." While some soldiers saw the spectacular aurora borealis as a sign that God was on the Union side, others took it as a sign of divine displeasure at the loss of so much life.

~ Aurora Borealis
Commemorative of the Dissolution of Armies
At the Peace
(May 1865)

Herman Melville

What power disbands the Northern Lights
    After their steely play?
The lonely watcher feels an awe
    Of Nature's sway,
        As when appearing,
        He marked their flashed uprearing
In the cold gloom –
    Retreatings and advancings,
(Like dallyings of doom),
        Transitions and enhancings,
        And bloody ray.

The phantom-host has faded quite,
    Splendour and Terror gone –
Portent or promise – and gives way
    To pale, meek Dawn;
        The coming, going,
        Alike in wonder showing –
Alike the God,
    Decreeing and commanding
The million blades that glowed,
        The muster and disbanding—
        Midnight and Morn.

Herman Melville (1819–1891) was a novelist, poet, and short-story writer. He was born and died in New York City to a family that had been active in the American Revolution and in the political development of the newly formed United States. Scarlet fever in his youth left him with diminished vision and, when his father died during his teens, Melville went to work to assist in supporting his family, first as a bank clerk and later as a farm hand and a cabin boy on a merchant ship. After a voyage to the South Seas aboard a whaler, he returned home and began to write. He volunteered for service in the Navy during the Civil War, but was rejected. During his lifetime, he enjoyed periods of acclaim but also periods in which his work was broadly rejected, during which time he worked for nineteen years as an inspector in a customs house in New York. The collection of poems from which the work above was drawn was written during the latter period.

From *Poems Containing Battle-Pieces, John Marr and Other Sailors, Timoleon, and Miscellaneous Poems* by Herman Melville. London: Constable and Company Ltd., 1924.

* * * * *

This poem was reprinted in *An Anthology of Revolutionary Poetry*. As you read this poem, you might consider what might have prompted the anthologist to deem it revolutionary.

~   **Freedom**

Isobel Luke

With head uplifted,
Saying my prayers unto the stars,
That I may advance into a new life,
Waking with flowers at dawn
Passing through the path of knowledge,
I make myself known unto myself,
A grafted branch of a storm-lashed tree,
Leaping with the growth of life,
Free from the brutal clasp of regret,
Through a forest of beauty,
Blazed with the stars of Hope,
Belted with a girdle of abundance,
The green lit grass spreading a carpet of silence,
As love trips down the world-wide street,
Letting down the everlasting bars of darkness,
Breaking the bonds of convention,
Blazing the trail of freedom,
I return to my task.
No longer shall I wear the garments of heaviness,
Dwelling in the imprisoned future,

Drinking from the black spring of death,
But breaking, restive, striving –
For the path of joy and song,
I march with the multitude
In search of understanding
Where the words Justice and Freedom
Are graven by the hand of time
On the heart of brotherhood.

Isobel Luke lived in Boston, Massachusetts and served in a number of leadership positions with the American Literary Association. The American Literary Association was based in Wauwatosa, Wisconsin and published *American Poetry Magazine*. In addition to being a poet, Luke was a leader in the organization; she was a life member of the A.L.A., president of the organization's Boston chapter and the chair of the Program Committee, and served as representative of the Massachusetts group and then all of New England. A 1923 issue of *American Poetry Magazine* indicates that she was "one of the first members to read her poems over the wireless under the auspices of the A.L.A." She was also the president of the American Poetry Association. She published a volume of poetry entitled, *Mother, Love, and Garden Poems* in 1921. This poem was originally published in *American Poetry Magazine*. Luke was also skilled in needlework, and her poem "Old Laces" is one of a very few of her poems that survives today.

Reprinted in *An Anthology of Revolutionary Poetry* by Marcus Graham, Ralph Cheyney & Lucia Trent. New York: The Active Press, Inc., 1929.

* * * * *

The following poem was inspired by the poet's time in India during the summer of 1982, as part of a Fulbright-Hays Foundation grant. In his introduction to the portion of the book *The Same Air* entitled, "Songs of India," the poet explains the reference that opens this poem, as follows: "As Guy Murchie in his wonderful book *The Seven Mysteries of Life* says, any human is no less than a fiftieth cousin of any other human, a millionth cousin to the great apes, and a quadrillionth cousin to the members of the mineral kingdom." As you read this poem, consider those words of connection and interdependence.

~   The Same Air

Al Zolynas

— for Guy Murchie,
The Seven Mysteries of Life

The same air
that moves
through me and you

through the waving branches
of the bronchial tree
through veins
through the heart
the same air
that fills balloons
that carries voices
full of lies and truths
and half-truths
that holds up the wings of butterflies
humming birds eagles hang gliders 747s
the same air
that sits like a dull relative
on humid lakes
in Minnesota in summer
the same air
trapped in vintage champagne
in old bicycle tires lost tennis balls
the air inside a vial in a sarcophagus
in a tomb in a pyramid
buried beneath the sand
the same air
inside your freezer
wrapping its cold arms
around your t.v. dinners
the same air that supports you
that supports me
the same air that moves through us
that we move through
the same air frogs creak with
cattle bellow with
monks meditate with and on
the same air we moan with
in pleasure or in pain

the breath I'm taking now
will be in China in two weeks
my lungs have passed an atom
of oxygen that passed through the lungs
of Socrates or Plato
or Lao-tsu or Buddha
or Walt Disney or Ronald Reagan
or a starving child in Somalia
or certainly you
you right here right now
yes certainly you
the same air
the very same air

Dr. Al Zolynas was born in Austria to a Lithuanian family in 1945. Growing up, he lived in Chicago and also in Sydney, Australia. He holds a Ph.D. in Creative Writing and English from the University of Utah. Now retired from teaching, Dr. Zolynas was a professor of literature and writing at both San Diego State University and Alliant International University. In addition to the numerous literary publications and anthologies in which Dr. Zolynas' work has appeared, he has also published four books of poetry: *The New Physics, Under Ideal Conditions, The Same Air*, and *Near and Far*. He is also a teacher of Zen meditation in Escondido, California, where he and his wife now live.

From *The Same Air: Poems of India* by Al Zolynas, *Paintings of India* by Netter Worthington, *Calligraphs and Illustrations* by Anwar Dil, with a foreword and collage of India by Donald E. Smith. San Diego: Intercultural Studies Forum, Inc., 1997.

∗   ∗   ∗   ∗   ∗

Wisdom is that freshness of mind which enables one to realise that truth is not hoarded in caskets of maxims, it is free and living.
— Rabindranath Tagore

As you read this poem, you might consider the way in which it reflects both truth and wisdom.

~   **35**

Rabindranath Tagore

Where the mind is without fear and the head is held high;
    Where knowledge is free;
    Where the world has not been broken up into fragments
by narrow domestic walls;
    Where words come out from the depth of truth;
    Where tireless striving stretches its arms towards perfection;
    Where the clear stream of reason has not lost its way into
the dreary desert sand of dead habit;
    Where the mind is led forward by thee into ever-widening
thought and action—
    Into that heaven of freedom, my Father, let my country
awake.

Rabindranath Tagore (1861–1941) was a prolific writer, famous both in his native Bengal (now West Bengal, India) and in the West. He won the Nobel Prize in Literature in 1913 for *Gitanjali*, becoming the first person from India to receive this honor. He began writing poetry at age eight and was greatly interested in social reform, including lending his support to the Indian nationalist movement; Tagore received a knighthood from Britain, from which he resigned to show his support for India following the 1919 Jallianwala Bagh massacre. His works include poems, songs, short stories, essays, novels, and dramas.

From *Gitanjali: A Collection of Prose Translations Made by the Author from the Original Bengali*, by Rabindranath Tagore. Macmillan Publishing Company, 1913.

* * * * *

The Cradle of Humankind is one of eight World Heritage sites in South Africa. The official government website indicates that it is widely recognized as having

> unearthed the best evidence of the complex journey that our species has taken to make us what we are—and is therefore a place of pilgrimage for all humankind. The area is not only a place of ongoing scientific discovery into our origins, but also a place of contemplation—a place that allows us to reflect on who we are, where we come from, and where we are going to.

~   In the cradle of humankind

Karen Press

Geological time locates us
at the crossroads of hominids and democracy,
wiser or younger or older or more harmonised
than the non-miraculous nations of the world.

We used to be teeth like grubby stones
packed solid in warm earth.
Our teeth were enough to tell
the fossilised story of our lives.

Something unearthed us,
broke us open, flung us out
into the big black nowhere of the universe.

Something rearranged the coal dust of our souls
so that we could have the momentary radiance of flowers,
and become rubies more precious than blood.

Karen Press is a South African poet, educator, and co-founder of Buchu Books, a publishing collective. She was born and lives in Cape Town. She has published ten collections of poetry, and her work has been published and anthologized in South Africa and around the world. In 2015, she was recognized with the South African Literary Awards' Literary Translators Award for her work in the translation of Afrikaans poetry. Carcanet Press, which has published three of Press's volumes of poetry, is itself a study in survival and persistence, having survived an IRA bomb at its Manchester headquarters in 1996 and having been lauded for making a concerted commitment to promote South African poetry.

From *The Canary's Songbook* by Karen Press. Manchester: Carcanet Press Ltd., 2005.

✶ ✶ ✶ ✶ ✶

Lines from this sonnet are displayed on the Statue of Liberty, on a plaque that was placed on the inner wall of the pedestal in 1903. The poem was written in 1883 as part of the "Art Loan Fund Exhibition in Aid of the Bartholdi Pedestal Fund for the Statue of Liberty." As the name suggests, this was a body of literary works auctioned off to raise the final sums of money that were needed for the Statue's pedestal.

~ The New Colossus

Emma Lazarus

Not like the brazen giant of Greek fame,
With conquering limbs astride from land to land;
Here at our sea-washed, sunset gates shall stand
A mighty woman with a torch, whose flame
Is the imprisoned lightning, and her name
Mother of Exiles. From her beacon-hand
Glows world-wide welcome; her mild eyes command
The air-bridged harbor that twin cities frame.
"Keep, ancient lands, your storied pomp!" cries she
With silent lips. "Give me your tired, your poor,
Your huddled masses yearning to breathe free,
The wretched refuse of your teeming shore.
Send these, the homeless, tempest-tost to me,
I lift my lamp beside the golden door!"

Emma Lazarus (1849–1887), was a poet of Portugese Sephardic Jewish descent. She was active in charitable work for refugees, in addition to her work as a poet. She began writing poetry in her teens and was mentored by Ralph Waldo Emerson after she sent him copies of her poems. Popular while alive, Lazarus's works were published in magazines and her own books. She is credited as having been one of the earliest successful and visible Jewish-American poets. She spoke out against the rise of antisemitism and was an early supporter of the concept of a Jewish homeland.

From *The Poems of Emma Lazarus, Volume 1.* New York: Houghton Mifflin Company, 1888.

✶ ✶ ✶ ✶ ✶

Permissions

Stephanie Burt, "The Body of the Poem," from the *Los Angeles Review of Books*. © 2013. Reprinted by permission of the *Los Angeles Review of Books*. This article was originally published in the Los Angeles Review of Books (www .lareviewofbooks.org).

Stephanie Burt, "Hermit Crab" from *Advice from the Lights*. Copyright © 2017 by Stephen Burt. Reprinted with the permission of The Permissions Company LLC on behalf of Graywolf Press, www.graywolfpress.org.

John Brandi, "Night Drive, After a Workshop at the State Pen," from *Hymn for a Night Feast: Poems: 1979–1986*. © 1996. Reprinted by permission of John Brandi.

Dee Allen, "Between Homes," from *Street Sheet*. © 2017. Reprinted by permission of Dee Allen.

Naomi Ortiz, "Ablesplaining Part 2,749," from *We Are Not Your Metaphor: A Disability Anthology*. © 2019. Reprinted by permission of Naomi Ortiz.

Michael J. Howlett, Jr., "2009 Criminal Docket," from 36 Legal Stud. F. (2012). © 2012. Reprinted by permission of Mrs. Kathleen Howlett.

Martín Espada, "Offerings to an Ulcerated God," from *Imagine the Angels of Bread*. © 1997. Reprinted by permission of Martín Espada.

Nancy A. Henry, "Baby's First Bath," from *Anything Can Happen*. © 2002. Reprinted by permission of MuscleHead Press.

Barbara Charline Jordan, quote from 1994 article in *On Campus Magazine*. © 1994. Reprinted by permission of Texas Student Media/On Campus.

Priscilla B. Adams, "School Bus Wreck," from *Poetry: Windows and Mirrors*. © 1995. Reprinted by permission of Lawrence, Clay, and Kristen Adams.

J.D. DuPuy & M.L. Philpott, "Vacation," from *Poetic Justice: Legal Humor in Verse*. © 2013. Reprinted by permission of J.D. DuPuy & M.L. Philpott.

Steven M. Richman, "Letters of Credit," from 36 Legal Stud. F. (2012). © 2012. Reprinted by permission of Steven M. Richman.

James Clarke, "Going Home," from *Flying Through the Dark*. © 2001. Reprinted by permission of Exile Editions.

About the Editor

Kristen David Adams has been a member of the faculty at Stetson University College of Law since 2000 and currently holds the William Reece Smith, Jr. Distinguished Professorship. She is the author or co-author of seven books and has also written more than twenty law review articles. Her three most recent books, *CISG Basics: A Guide to International Sales Law* (with Candace Zierdt), *The ABCs of the UCC: Related and Supplementary Consumer Law, Third Edition* (with Candace Zierdt), and *Law and Poetry: Promises from the Preamble*, were published by the American Bar Association.

Adams is an elected member of the American Law Institute, a member of Council for the American Bar Association Business Law Section and a former chair of the Uniform Commercial Code Committee, a member of the American Bar Association Commission on Homelessness and Poverty, an officer and fellow of the American College of Commercial Finance Lawyers, the American Bar Association Business Law Section's Liaison to the Permanent Editorial Board for the Uniform Commercial Code, and the current chair of the board for Gulfcoast Legal Services.

At Stetson, she teaches courses in property, domestic and international commercial law, and law through the lens of poetry. She is the faculty director for the College of Law's Dispute Resolution Board and one of the faculty coordinators for the Social Justice Advocacy Concentration. She earned her B.A. from Rice University, her J.D. from Emory Law School, and her LL.M. from Yale Law School. She practiced law in Atlanta with Alston & Bird LLP and Altman, Kritzer & Levick, P.C. before she became a professor.